...and on a mount, all of grated Parmesan cheese, dwelt folk that do naught else but make maccheroni and ravioli and boil them in capon's broth, and then throw them down to be scrambled for; and hard by flows a rivulet of Vernaccia, the best that ever was drunk, and never a drop of water therein.

Giovanni Boccaccio, *Decameron*

Sandra Rosi

FLORENCE

The Art of Cookery

Illustrated by Paola Boldrini

Mandragora

© 2001 Mandragora. All rights reserved.
Piazza Duomo, 9 - 50122 Firenze
Graphic design: *Lorenzo Gualtieri*
Translation: *Eve Leckey*
Illustrated by *Paola Boldrini*
Colour separation: *Studio Leonardo* - Firenze
Printed by *Alpilito* - Firenze
ISBN   88-85957-14-5

This book is printed on TCF
(*totally chlorine free*) paper

▼

The recipes in this Florentine cookery book range from the original and traditional to more recent arrivals and innovations. Such a wide and occasionally unusual choice of dishes has not only provided some fascinating historical and social information, but the assortment and variety of flavours, colours, customs and costs suited to all pockets, also offers a style of cooking which is lively and flexible. Three essential elements have formed our gastronomic traditions: the 'poor', peasant tradition with the emphasis on bread soups, vegetables, beans and eggs, with very little meat (beef was rare but there was sometimes pork, rabbit and chicken and, just occasionally, a poached hare); the cookery of the middle-classes, which probably is most similar to today's in tastes and cost and includes a bit of everything (varied and flavoursome dishes with spices, herbs and a choice of wines); the cookery of the aristocracy which, after the marriage of Catherine de' Medici to the Dauphin, Henry of Orleans in 1533, heavily influenced French cookery. Not surprizingly I have had to tone down or vary some flavours which were too strong or even unacceptable to the modern palate, while, on the other hand, I have made use of some ingredients which were previously unknown or only rarely used, - interesting and lively cookery depends on its ability to evolve and absorb new ideas and preferences. Indeed, the most creative and inventive cooking develops in the home and trattoria as it is here that traditional dishes are continually renewed and updated with those small but important additions and adjustments.

▼

At the heart of Florentine cookery lie three fundamental ingredients: bread (plain, unsalted, well-baked with a crispy crust and light and airy inside); extra-virgin olive oil, without any doubt the best even for frying, as long as you only use it once; lastly, wine, and being a genuine wine enthusiast, I have dedicated a separate section to it. Clearly the success of such a simple and natural style of cooking depends to a great extent on the freshness and quality of the ingredients. This is especially important for vegetables and salad which, if left in the fridge for too long, will loose both their flavour and their vitamin content.

The quantities given in the recipes are for a convivial gathering of six people and each includes instructions, equipment and timing as well as some interesting traditions and customs. To save time, there is absolutely no reason why you should not use a pressure cooker, mixer, pasta maker or any other machine which makes life easier. On the other hand, avoid at all costs pre-cooked or ready-prepared foods, tinned beans and frozen foods, while the stock cube should only be used as a last resort.

Salse e Sughi

Sauces

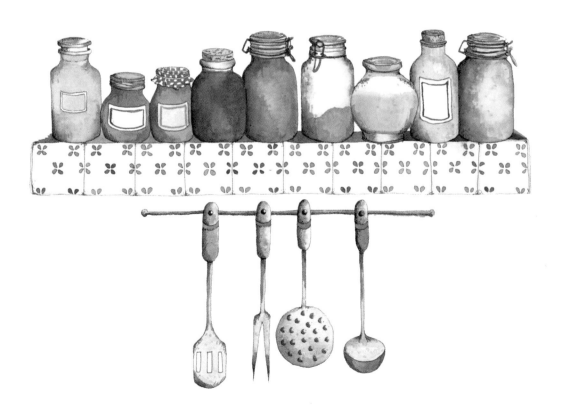

The earliest texts on Italian cookery

While researching into the origins of Florentine cookery, I came across several fascinating, authoritative texts on gastronomy written by experts over the centuries. The oldest account that I found dates back to the first century A.D. and is a manual written in Latin and entitled *De re coquinaria* by Marco Gavio, better known as Apicius (a famous gourmand of the first century B.C.) Many centuries passed however between this first recipe book and the other writers mentioned in the recipes. At the very end of the fourteenth century and beginning of the fifteenth century the *Anonimo Toscano* (The Anonymous Tuscan) collected a series of recipes together in his book, the *Libro della cocina* (Book of Cooking). Unfortunately he was somewhat imprecise in his descriptions, which lacked much rather useful information (such as the quantities!). Such necessary details were provided instead by Maestro Martino in his *Libro de arte coquinaria* (The Book of Culinary Art). Written in the vernacular and dated 1450, this book provides a minute description of every aspect of the art of cooking. Maestro Martino was much appreciated by Bartolomeo Sacchi, otherwise known as *Il Platina*, (1421-1481) and in his *De honesta voluptate et valetudine*, he translated the Maestro's texts into Latin with various additions and comments of his own. Several texts on cookery appeared during the sixteenth century: in 1549 Cristoforo Messi Sbugo wrote *Banchetti, composizioni di vivandi et apparecchio generale* (Banquets, the arrangment of foods and general equipment), while in 1560 Domenico Romoli, known as *Panunto*, published *La singolar dottrina...* (the Unusual Doctrine...). Although the former lived and worked in Ferrara and the latter in Florence, both men were stewards (originally it was they who ordered the meals and carved) at grand and important courts. In these manuals they explain the art and conventions of dining and feasting. Pietro Mattioli wrote his *Commentarii in sex libros Pedacii...* (Pedacius' commentary in six books...) in 1565, and in 1581 Vincenzo Cervio wrote *Il Trinciante* (The Carver), the first text to describe how to carve and cut food, which knives to use and how to look after their blades. At the end of the last century Pellegrino Artusi wrote *La scienza in cucina e l'arte di mangiar bene* (Science in the kitchen and the art of good food), an almost definitive compendium of the recipes, hints, ideas and customs relating to Italian cookery and passed down throughout the centuries.

▼

Burro e salvia

Sage and butter

Wash and dry the sage leaves. Melt the butter in a saucepan and add the sage. Cook very gently over a low flame taking care not to let the butter burn. Pour over cooked pasta and stir through well together with freshly grated parmesan. This super-quick sauce is ideal with 'naked ravioli' (ravioli filling without the pasta) but it is also suitable with any short pasta. In this case, drain the cooked pasta keeping back a little of the water. Return the pasta to the saucepan, add the sage and butter and stir over a low heat for a minute.

Remove from the heat and stir in a good helping of grated Parmesan.

The sauce should look smooth and creamy; if it has dried out too much, add a few drops of milk or fresh cream. Grind a little black pepper over when serving.

Preparation time:
5 minutes.
Cooking time:
5 minutes.
100 g butter
bunch of fresh sage leaves
80 g grated
Parmesan
black pepper.

▼

Salsa di pomodoro

Tomato sauce I

Preparation time:
10 minutes.
Cooking time:
20 minutes.
500 g tomatoes
4 tbsp extra-virgin
olive oil
one onion
salt
basil.

Peel and chop the tomatoes. Peel and finely chop the onion. Put the oil in a large frying pan and fry the onion. Cook for about five minutes and then add the chopped tomatoes and a pinch or two of salt. Increase the heat and cook for another ten minutes. When you have removed the sauce from the heat, add the fresh basil leaves. This sauce is delicious in the summer time when plump, delicious tomatoes are readily available, and is suitable for all kinds of pasta. Remember to provide grated Parmesan for those who wish.

This sauce can also be used as a dressing for cold pasta. In this case try adding some chopped, diced mozzarella to the cold sauce; this lends a wonderfully fresh, tangy flavour to the dish.

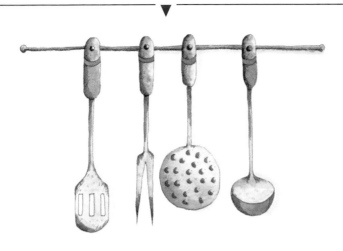

Sugo di pomodoro

Tomato sauce II

Peel and chop the tomatoes. Put the oil and whole garlic cloves in a saucepan and cook over a medium heat until the cloves begin to brown.

Add the tomatoes and cook for fifteen minutes. Remove the garlic cloves and add a good handful of fresh basil leaves.

This sauce is perfect with a dash of chili pepper which should be served, either powdered or crushed, at the table with the pasta. If you like to flavour your pasta with cheese, try either a mature pecorino or salty, hard ricotta, both freshly grated at the table.

The best time of year to make tomato sauce is in the summer when when plump, ripe, juicy tomatoes full of flavour are abundant.

Penne are the most suitable form of pasta with this sauce. If, however, you have the time and patience to make your own pasta, then try it with taglierini, rolled out to a thickness of about two millimetres.

Preparation time:
10 minutes.
Cooking time:
20 minutes.
500 g ripe tomatoes
4 tbsp extra-virgin
olive oil
4 cloves of garlic
fresh basil
salt
chili pepper.

Ragù di carne alla fiorentina

Florentine meat sauce

*Preparation time:
15 minutes.
Cooking time:
50 minutes.
One onion
one carrot
one stick of celery
parsley
4 tbsp extra-virgin
olive oil
300 g minced meat
100 g chicken or
rabbit livers
one glass red wine
700 g tomatoes
salt.*

Finely chop the onion, carrot, celery and parsley. Fry gently in the oil over a medium heat.

Add the minced meat (do not use mince which is too lean!) and the washed and cleaned livers, finely chopped.

Add salt and cook rapidly for at least ten minutes, stirring constantly with a wooden spoon so that the meat does not stick to the pan.

When the sauce has become golden brown in colour, add the wine and leave to evaporate. Lower the heat and add the peeled and puréed tomatoes. Cook over a low heat for half an hour and taste for salt. You could serve

this sauce with chili pepper. The method I have described here produces a fairly liquid, but very light sauce. If you prefer it thicker, simply cook it for two hours instead: this produces an entirely different consistency and flavour.

Sugo finto

Rich tomato sauce

Pour the oil into a large saucepan and warm over a low heat without letting it begin to smoke.

Chop the onion, carrot and celery and fry gently together in the oil. Peel and roughly chop the tomatoes and add to the fried ingredients when they become soft and light golden. Increase the heat and cook for ten minutes.

On removing from the heat, add a handful of chopped parsley and stir in well. Make sure to provide freshly grated Parmesan when serving the pasta. If you wish to give the sauce a bit more flavour, fry the bacon, chopped and diced, with the onion, celery and carrot.

This sauce is good with maccheroncini, both smooth and grooved, and was traditionally considered a 'poor' dish as it contains no meat. Indeed the recipe is identical to a meat-based ragù, - without the meat!

Preparation time:
15 minutes.
Cooking time:
20 minutes.
One onion
one carrot
one stick of celery
parsley
4 tbsp extra-virgin
olive oil
700 g tomatoes
salt
100 g streaky bacon
(unsmoked).

▼

Salsa verde

Green sauce

*Preparation time:
15 minutes.
Cooking time:
7 minutes.
Standing time:
30 minutes.
One egg
a good handful of
fresh parsley
300 g bread
teaspoon of
wine vinegar
5 tbsp extra-virgin
olive oil
salt.
Optional:
one anchovy fillet
one garlic clove
black pepper.*

Boil the egg for seven minutes, leave it to cool and remove the shell. Mash it with a fork in a small bowl, working it until quite smooth and creamy. Remove the stems from the parsley and chop the leaves finely; add to the mashed egg. Soak the bread, with the crusts removed, to soften it (use unsalted bread, a day or two old), squeeze the water out, crumble it finely and add to the other ingredients. Sprinkle with the oil and vinegar and beat the mixture together thoroughly, adding a pinch of salt. Leave in a cool place or in the fridge for at least 30 minutes and pour into a sauce boat before serving. This sauce is the classic accompaniment for boiled meats and several versions of it exist. The most frequent variation is simply with a dash of pepper; those who prefer a stronger flavour can also add a chopped or grated clove of garlic to the mixture, while 'extremists' like an anchovy fillet, mashed together with the egg.

This recipe has been known and handed down in various forms for centuries. Bartolomeo Sacchi wrote of it "...this sauce has little nutritional value, it inflames the stomach and the liver and it is difficult to digest. However, it has the merit of loosening the bowel and stimulating the appetite".

▼

Besciamella

Béchamel sauce

Melt the butter over a low heat in a stainless steel pan. Gradually sprinkle in the flour, and stir well with a wooden spoon until smooth in consistency; cook gently until the mixture becomes a light golden colour. Add the milk gradually, stirring constantly to avoid lumps forming. Should this occur, you will have to sieve the sauce. Cook for at least fifteen minutes stirring all the time. When the béchamel becomes rich and creamy in consistency - not too thick and not too runny, but forming ribbons on the surface when it falls from the spoon - remove from the heat, taste for salt, add a pinch of powdered nutmeg and the grated Parmesan. For a different flavour, you can replace the milk with the same quantity of beef stock, or use half milk and half stock.

The famous Italian cookery writer, Pellegrino Artusi affirmed that "A good béchamel and a well thickened meat sauce are the basis and the greatest secret of good cookery", and there is a lot of truth in the statement...

Ironically, béchamel sauce was probably re-introduced to Italy from France. In fact, the original 'Biancomangiare' (White pudding), which is a sweet variation made with ground almonds, dates back to Maestro Martino, and was later revived by Bartolomeo Sacchi.

Preparation time:
5 minutes.
Cooking time:
15 minutes.
50 g butter
2 tbsp plain flour
half a litre milk
50 g Parmesan
nutmeg
salt.
Optional:
half a litre beef stock.

Setting the table

The famous French gourmet, Anthelme Brillat-Savarin, maintained that "Inviting a guest into our home means being responsible for their happiness for the entire duration of their stay". To be completely successful in this, not only is it important to satisfy our guest's palate by preparing the choicest of foods, but also to provide a pleasant setting, attractively decorated with little, artistic touches. Even if the meal is not a special occasion it should still be relaxed, cheerful and enjoyable.

Here are ten fundamental rules concerning the setting of the table, based on common sense as well as correct etiquette.

1. The tablecloth and serviettes should always be snow white, or perhaps pastel coloured, to provide a simple background on which to present the delicious food.

2. The glasses should always be clear and uncoloured, so that one can appreciate the colour of the wine.

3. The dinner plates, whether elegant or everyday, white or coloured, should not be highly decorated: one really cannot appreciate the appearance of the food, which is just as important as the flavour, if it is surrounded by complicated patterns.

4. A few flowers really do make your table look as pretty as a picture. Be careful though not to turn it into a jungle: remember that you do want to talk to your guests, and should therefore avoid creating a barrier between them and you.

5. Candlelight adds to the intimacy of a supper. The size and style of the candlesticks depends on the occasion itself, but they should never be too grandiose, unless you happen to live in a castle.

6. Whether silver, stainless steel or coloured, precise rules govern the placing of the cutlery. Starting with those furthest out, one works inwards. The knife and soup spoon are set on the right of the plate with the cutting edge of the knife turned inwards. The fork is on the left with the serviette beside it. Above the plate, perpendicular to the rest, are the dessert knife and fork: first the knife with the handle turned to the right and the blade towards the plate; immediately above is the fork, with the handle turned

towards the left. If a spoon is also required it can either be brought to the table with the dessert, or may be placed above the fork, with the handle to the right.

7. Glasses are placed to the right of the plate, in decreasing order of size: water, wine and lastly dessert wine. The dessert and the glass for the accompanying wine may also be brought to the table together.

8. If you like to provide a bread plate, this should be placed to the left of the fork.

9. If you are serving antipasti, provide a side plate on top of the dinner plate. If beginning with pasta, put a pasta dish on top of the dinner plate.

10. At the end of a course, plates are removed from the left and clean plates arc offered from the right.

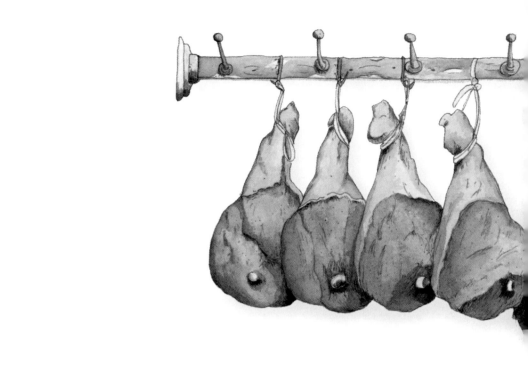

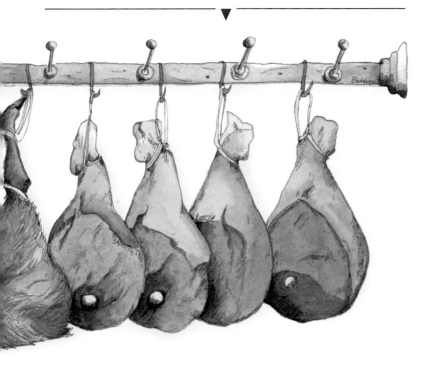

Antipasti

The antipasti

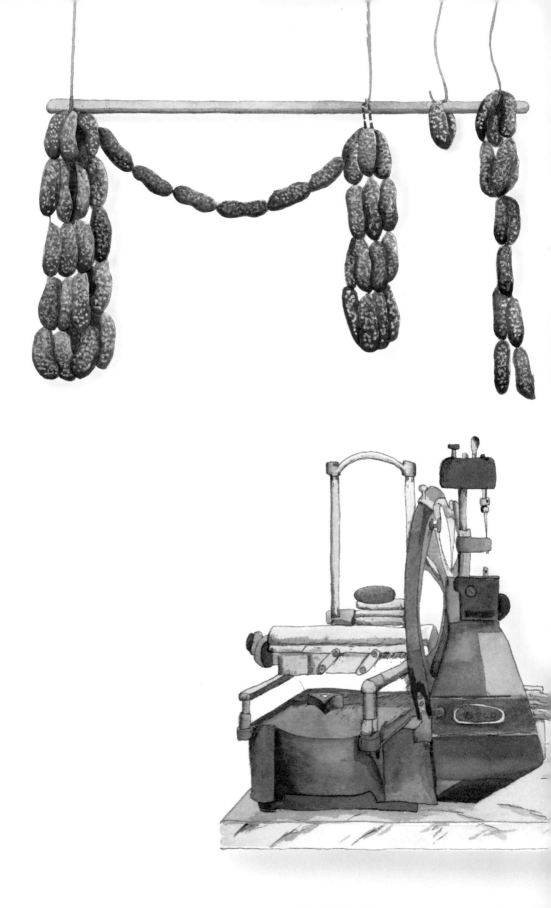

▼

Affettati misti

Cold sliced meats

This is one of the most traditional antipasti served in Florentine restaurants. In the home, an assortment of cold sliced meats was generally only served on important or festive occasions. Depending on the season, the meats were often served with fresh or mature pecorino, ricotta or raveggiolo cheeses, fresh raw beans or figs. Given its simplicity, it is essential that all the ingredients are fresh and of the best quality. Arrange the meats in circles on a serving dish and decorate with crisp, tangy salad leaves. Serve the bread, sliced about a centimetre thick, in a basket. The best wine to drink with these cold meats is a young and fairly light Chianti, such as that from the 'Colli fiorentini'.

Preparation time:
5 minutes.
200 g prosciutto ham
200 g finocchiona
200 g soprassata
(or 400 g assorted salamis
and cold meats)
400 g bread
a few salad leaves.

▼

Baccelli e pecorino

Young broad beans and pecorino cheese

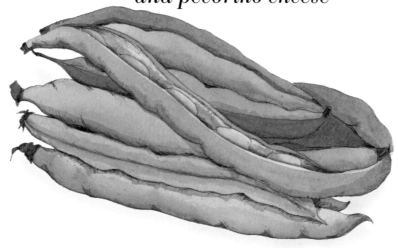

*Preparation time:
30 minutes.
Standing time:
one hour.
3 kg fresh, young broad
beans in their pods
400 g fresh pecorino
extra-virgin olive oil
salt
black pepper.*

Shell the beans, place in a salad bowl and dress with the oil, salt and pepper. Chop soft, young pecorino cheese into cubes (mature pecorino would overwhelm the delicate flavour of the broad beans) and add to the salad bowl. Leave aside in a cool place for an hour to let the flavours mingle. Serve with wholemeal bread.

This could also be an excellent main course, especially if you have already eaten a substantial first course and in the summer time it is also suitable as a quick lunch if you like broad beans and are not satisfied by the small portion of an antipasto.

Formaggio con le pere

Pears and cheese

Wash and peel the pears. Cut into cubes and place in a salad bowl, taking care not to loose any of the juice. Dice the pecorino and add to the chopped fruit. Mix together and leave to stand for ten minutes before serving. If desired, finely grind some black pepper over the top. Remember though, that pears and cheese as a starter will stimulate both appetite and taste buds, so this is best for those who are not watching their weight. Even if you are worried about the waistline though, don't deny yourself this delicious combination, you can still enjoy it but as a main course.

Preparation time:
20 minutes.
Standing time:
10 minutes.
6 firm pears
400 g pecorino cheese
black pepper.

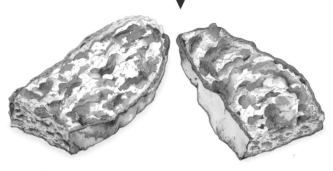

Crostini con salsiccia

Crostini with sausagemeat

Preparation time:
15 minutes.
Cooking time:
15 minutes.
3 salsicce (fresh Italian pork sausages)
*300 g *stracchino cheese*
12 slices unsalted country bread.
**stracchino is a sharp-flavoured creamy, spreading cheese*

Remove the skin from the sausages; place the meat in a large bowl and combine with the stracchino, working them together until smooth with a wooden spoon. Cut a dozen or so slices of bread about a centimetre thick and put in the oven for ten minutes, until crisp on both sides. Remove from the oven and allow to cool, then spread some of the mixture on each slice. Put back in the oven for five minutes and serve the crostini hot.

Do ensure that the sausages are entirely pure pork and that they are not seasoned, as these have an entirely different flavour.

▼

Crostini di fegato

Chicken liver crostini

Cut the onion into rings and fry in the oil with the chopped carrot and celery. Clean and wash the chicken livers, chop them roughly, add to the fried ingredients and brown well. If they dry out too much, moisten with a little stock or white wine, but allow it to evaporate well. Cook for twenty minutes, then remove from heat. Add the capers, anchovy fillets, chopped sage leaves and butter. Using a large kitchen knife, chop the entire mixture very finely. Lightly toast the slices of bread and spread with the liver paste. If the slices of bread are crisped under a grill, they may be moistened with a spoonful of stock before spreading with the liver mixture. I like my crostini crispy, however, so prefer not to do so.

The liver paste could also be served in an attractive bowl, surrounded with crisply toasted bread and decorated with herbs. Originally this spread was called *peverada* and was made using saffron which was widely grown in the countryside around the city.

Preparation time:
20 minutes.
Cooking time:
20 minutes.
One carrot
one onion
one stick of celery
3 tbsp extra-virgin
olive oil
300 g chicken livers
white wine or stock
one dessert spoon capers
4 anchovy fillets
freshly chopped sage
50 g butter
salt
500 g unsalted bread.

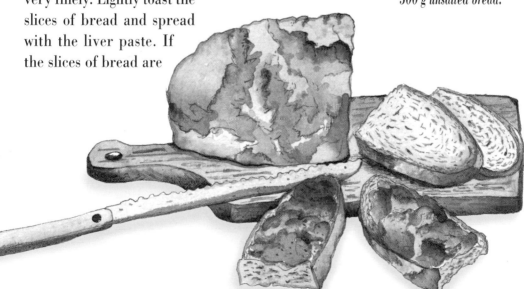

▼

Salvia fritta

Fried sage leaves

Preparation time:
20 minutes.
Cooking time:
20 minutes.
A bunch of fresh
sage leaves
anchovy fillets
batter
extra-virgin olive oil
salt.

Select the largest of the sage leaves and wash and dry them carefully. Sandwich two at a time together with an anchovy fillet in the middle. Press together and dip into the batter mix. Fry in the hot oil, and leave to dry on kitchen paper. Serve just warm. The medicinal properties of the sage plant have long been known, and the leaves are renowned for their beneficial effect on tooth enamel. The leaves used in this recipe should be young and fresh; the best time to pick them is in late spring when they have just newly sprouted.

In 1545, Cosimo I founded the Giardino dei Semplici (Botanical and Herb Garden) so that the plants and aromatic herbs used both for cooking and for medicinal purposes would always be readily available. It still exists today in Via La Pira and is open to the public.

Tonno e fagioli

Tuna and bean salad

Put the beans in approximately two and a half litres of cold, salted water with the garlic and sage and cook over a low heat for about one hour. Drain well. Arrange on the plates with the tuna fish. Dress with the oil and season with pepper. The dish can also be decorated with crisp, raw onion rings or sprinkled with a handful of capers, which should be well drained of the vinegar as the acidity might spoil the delicate balance of flavours. This dish is also suitable as a main course to follow a rather filling starter or pasta dish, or it may also be served as a handy, quick lunch. It is best served with crispy, wholemeal bread.

Cannellini beans are a speciality of Florentine cooking: they are a delicacy, fresh, in late summer. Florentines adore and eat all kinds of beans, indeed, long before the discovery of America the variety known as the 'black-eyed bean' was grown in the surrounding

Preparation time:
10 minutes.
Cooking time:
1 hour.
500 g fresh cannellini beans
sage
200 g tuna fish in oil
garlic
salt
black pepper
extra-virgin olive oil.
Optional:
fresh onion
pickled capers

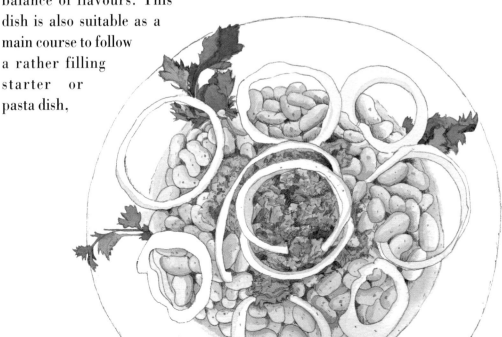

▼

Pinzimonio

Fresh vegetables with olive oil

Preparation time:
20 minutes.
Celery
carrots
fennel bulbs
cauliflower florets
baby cabbage leaves
spring onions
artichokes
extra-virgin olive oil
salt
black pepper.

The success of this simple and tasty dish depends on two fundamental elements: fresh, young ingredients and, above all, superb olive oil from the hills of Tuscany. Carefully clean all the vegetables, cut them into pieces and arrange on a serving platter. Each guest should have a small bowl containing the oil, salt and pepper into which he can dip the pieces of vegetables. Pinzimonio is an excellent appetizer and can be varied according to the season and the availablity of vegetables. How- ever, in late May, when the tender, sharp young, deep purple artichokes called *morellini* are available in Florence, this may be served either as an antipasto, or as a light main course. It is also a satisfying complete lunch for anyone on a diet. The artichokes may also be prepared on their own in a salad: slice very finely, flavour and dress with oil, salt and pepper and top with flakes of fresh Parmesan. Interestingly, in the past, artichokes were served as a dessert.

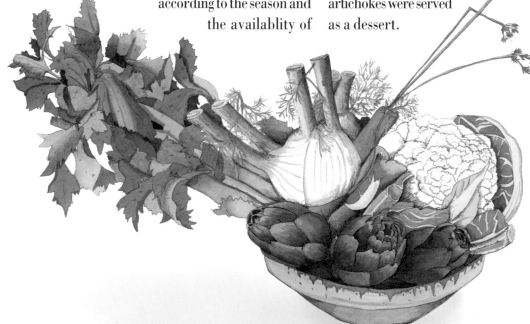

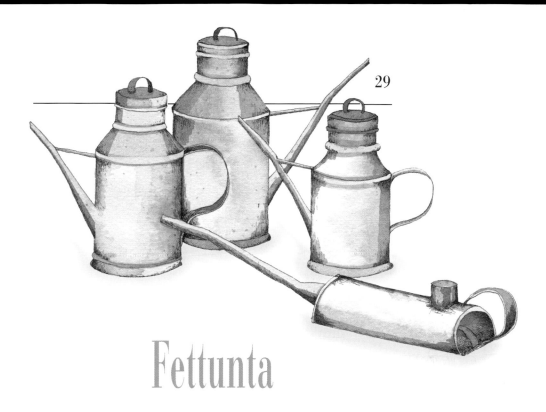

Fettunta

Toasted bread with olive oil

This dish is generally associated with the month of November, when the olives have been gathered and the oil is newly pressed. Obviously it is eaten all year round, but in other seasons it lacks that characteristic pungent flavour of the new oil. Cut the bread about a centimetre thick, grill well on both sides and rub one side generously with a clove of garlic. You just have to forget the unpleasant effect on your breath, if you are going to enjoy this properly: semel in anno licet insanire, as Dante once said, "everyone can go mad at least once a year". Place the slices on a large serving platter and drizzle the oil over them. Season with salt and pepper and eat while still hot. In the summer you can top the crostini with chopped tomatoes, or tomato sauce. In winter, fettunta is the basis of a traditional soup known, somewhat inexplicably, as 'Lombard soup': place the slice of bread in a soup bowl and cover with boiled cannellini beans, adding a little of the thick liquid in which they were cooked. Season with oil, salt and pepper.

Preparation time:
10 minutes.
Cooking time:
10 minutes.
Bread
extra-virgin olive oil
garlic
salt
black pepper.

▼

Pane dorato

Golden fried bread

Preparation time:
10 minutes.
Cooking time:
5 minutes.
6 slices of bread half a
centimetre thick
250 ml. milk
2 eggs, beaten
extra-virgin olive oil
salt
Optional:
100 g Gruyère cheese.

Half fill a heavy iron frying pan with oil. Cut the crusts off the bread and soak briefly in the milk. Dip both sides of each slice of bread into the beaten eggs. Heat the oil and plunge the slices into the pan one by one, frying each side for two minutes until golden brown. Remove from the pan and leave to drain on kitchen paper. Sprinkle with salt and serve hot. Sandwich bread is best for this recipe, as the result is lighter. It is even tastier if very finely cut slices of Gruyère cheese are laid on top of the freshly fried bread so that they gently melt into it. Golden fried bread can also be used to great effect in soups. Cut the slices into cubes and place in the soup dishes before serving clear beef broth at table. A historic cookery book compiled by

Domenico Romoli contains a recipe for *Pan dorato con butirro* (butter) but, in keeping with Renaissance and medieval tastes, the croutons were flavoured with sugar and cinnamon.

▼

Torta salata

Savoury flan

Work the flour, water, oil and salt together to form a smooth dough. Leave to rest for half an hour, then roll out and use to line a buttered flan dish. You can use almost any kind of vegetable for the filling, such as leeks, onions, chard, spinach or whatever is available. Wash, clean, drain and chop, add to the diced bacon and fry in the melted butter.

Beat the eggs and add the grated Parmesan with a pinch of nutmeg and salt. Off the heat, stir into the fried vegetables and then pour into the lined flan dish. Bake in the oven at 180° for thirty minutes. Before bringing to the table, wash and dry some leaves of parsley and arrange them on top of the flan in an attractive flower pattern.

In the words of Domenico Romoli, "A vegetable tart…cook it the way you cook tarts".

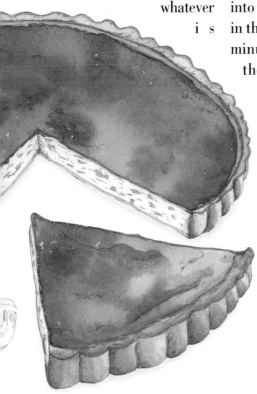

Preparation time:
15 minutes.
Standing time:
30 minutes.
Cooking time:
30 minutes.
300 g plain flour
250 ml water
3 tbsp extra-virgin
olive oil
pinch salt
500 g leeks
(or onions, Swiss chard or
other vegetable)
100 g streaky bacon
20 g butter
2 eggs
100 g Parmesan
nutmeg
salt.

▼

Raveggiolo

Home-made cream cheese

Preparation time: 10 minutes.
Standing time: 20 hours.
One litre milk
rennet
rocket salad leaves
extra-virgin olive oil
vinegar
salt.

Add the rennet to the milk, stir in well and pour into a large soup tureen, lined with fine muslin. Leave to stand for at least twenty hours and when the mixture has become fairly thick and solid in consistency, use the muslin to lift it out of the bowl. Let all the water drain away and turn the cheese out onto a serving platter. Add salt and serve garnished with leaves of rocket, tossed in a dressing of oil, vinegar and salt.

Raveggiola requires either cow or goat's milk, taken straight from the animal and thus not subjected to industrial heat treatment. It really is worth the time and effort involved in preparing this delicious soft cheese to savour its delicately sharp flavour. This is a good dish to accompany a summer evening's dinner. Raveggiola was often made into smaller forms and left to mature for several months. If you have a cool, well-aired and dry cellar, you could try this too: the forms should be set on wooden planks so that the cheese can 'breath' properly. In the past raveggiolo was known as *giuncata* (giunco = rushes) after the little plaited rush baskets in which it was left to thicken. In fact the *Anonimo Toscano* gives us a recipe entitled *'De la ioncada'*.

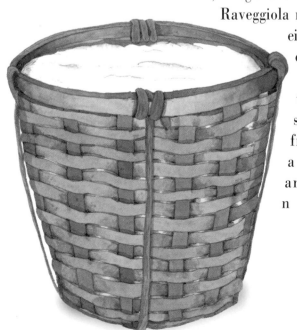

Primi piatti

First Courses

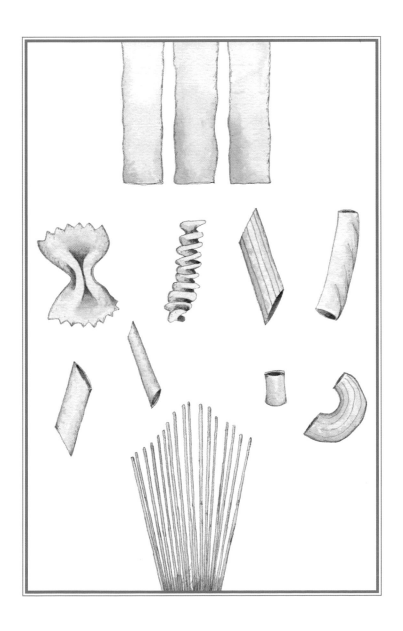

How to cook pasta

Depending on the creativity of the cook and the ingredients used, pasta can be served in an infinite variety of ways. When cooking it however, some basic rules must always be followed:

1. Pasta should always be cooked in a large saucepan with abundant water (one litre for every 100g of pasta).
2. Salt the water when it comes to the boil (10g salt for every litre of water), wait for it to come to the boil again and drop in the pasta.
3. Stir with a wooden spoon immediately after adding the pasta to the water, to stop it sticking to the bottom of the pan.

4. If using fresh pasta, it is a good idea to add a teaspoon of extra-virgin olive oil to prevent it sticking.

5. Cook over a medium heat with the lid set half on to prevent the water boiling over.

6. Drain the pasta when it is 'al dente' (firm to the bite). Ravioli should be removed with a skimmer as each one rises to the surface. Never leave the pasta sitting in the warm water as it will continue to cook. Drain thoroughly if transferring straight to the pasta plates; save a little of the cooking water if it has to be tossed in a pan or mixed with the sauce in a serving bowl. The cooking water is most useful for diluting a sauce which is too thick or when combining the pasta with a sauce by tossing or stirring them together over heat, as it prevents the fats frying for too long.

7. If cooking dried spaghetti or taglierini made with egg, never snap or break them; drop them into the saucepan (which should be high-sided) and push down into the water as they gradually soften.

8. The type of pasta used usually depends on the sauce to be served: fresh pasta, especially if thin-cut, is best suited to delicate sauces such as those based on butter, cream, vegetables, herbs or fish; dry pasta is better for stronger and thicker sauces. Let your own tastes and instincts guide you however, though remember that the classic hare sauce with pappardelle (broad noodles) is the exception that proves the rule.

Pasta fresca

Fresh pasta

Preparation time:
20 minutes.
Standing time:
20 minutes.
600 g plain flour, sifted
3 eggs
teaspoon extra-virgin
olive oil
salt.

Pile the flour onto a clean work surface. Make a well in the middle and break the eggs into it, together with the oil, salt and 10 ml of water. Use a fork to break the eggs and gradually beat them into the flour then, using your hands, knead gently until the dough is soft and elastic. Make it into a ball, cover and leave aside for ten minutes. Clean the work surface completely, dust it with flour and roll the pasta out with a long rolling pin. If you roll the dough out in a circular shape it will be easier to maintain an even thickness of about one millimetre. Leave to rest for ten minutes and then cut into strips thirty centimetres wide. Make these into a roll, folding them over widthwise four times. Use a large, sharp knife to cut them into the shape or size desired: pappardelle are 2.5cm wide, maccheroni 1.5cm, tagliatelle 5mm and taglierini 2mm. The rolling pin should be about a metre long and the working surface or board on which the pasta is rolled out should be wide, smooth and wooden.

To quote the *Anonimo Toscano*: "For lasagne. Take some good white flour; sprinkle with tepid water…". And from Maestro Martino: "Maccaroni…make the pasta a bit thicker than for lasagne, and wind it around a stick…".

▼

Crespelle

Crêpes

Beat the eggs and stir in the salt, milk, melted butter and flour. Mix well, grease a small frying pan and pour in one ladleful of batter at a time. Cook well until golden on both sides. Prepare the filling as follows: clean and wash the spinach, cook in a little salted, boiling water for ten minutes. Allow to drain well, squeeze out excess water and chop finely. Mix together in a bowl with the beaten egg, parmesan, ricotta, some salt and a pinch of nutmeg. Fill the crepes, roll up and arrange in a buttered, oven-proof dish. Pour over a béchamel sauce and top with Parmesan cheese. Cook in the oven at 180° for fifteen minutes. Check they are crisp and brown on top before removing. Both ravioli and crespelle are dishes typically used to replace meat and are therefore often served on Fridays and during Lent.

Preparation time:
30 minutes.
Cooking time:
45 minutes.
To make ten crêpes:
3 eggs
400 ml milk
30 g butter
120 g plain flour
salt.
For the filling:
one kg young spinach leaves
250 g ricotta
one egg
50 g Parmesan
salt
pinch of nutmeg.

▼

Carabaccia

Sweet onion soup

Preparation time:
20 minutes.
Cooking time:
40 minutes.
100 g blanched almonds
150 ml white wine vinegar
cinnamon stick
one kg onions
4 tbsp extra-virgin
olive oil
teaspoon sugar
one litre stock
6 slices of bread
Gruyère cheese
salt.

Crush the almonds in a mortar and leave them to soak in the vinegar with the cinnamon stick for about one hour. Finely chop the onions and fry in the oil. Rinse the almonds in a sieve and add to the onions. Add the sugar, salt and stock and cook for half an hour. Toast the slices of bread, place a slice in each dish and pour over the onion soup. You could garnish the soup by sprinkling grated Gruyère cheese over just before serving, or even return it to the oven for ten minutes, with the cheese on top. Onions are one of the basic ingredients in all Italian cooking and even the ancient Etruscans were aware of their medicinal properties, especially for c u r i n g inflamation. The Roman cook, Apicius, (Ist century A.D.) used them in a recipe for hot broth. According to Bartolomeo Sacchi, they "...encourage lust, their strong, agreeable flavour favouring its impulses...". This dish was very popular during the Middle Ages and the Renaissance, and is mentioned by both the *Anonimo Tos-cano* and Cristoforo di Messi

Zuppa di cipolle

Onion soup

Slice the onion into fine rings and fry gently in the butter in a flameproof earthenware dish. Stir with a wooden spoon to avoid the onion sticking. Continue stirring while gradually sprinkling in the flour. Slowly add the warm stock and blend in thoroughly. Cook for twenty minutes and taste for salt towards the end.

Arrange the slices of toasted bread (use unsalted, country bread) in an ovenproof dish and pour the soup over. Grate, or slice the Gruyère or Fontina very finely and arrange evenly over the top. Put in the oven at 180° until it melts and serve when golden brown and crisp.

According to the great expert, Artusi, this soup can be made with either stock or milk; you could try both to see which you prefer. If liked, you could also replace the flour with 300g of peeled and diced potatoes.

Preparation time:
20 minutes.
Cooking time:
30 minutes.
One kg onions
80 g butter
40 g flour
1 litre stock
250 g bread
100 g Gruyère
or Fontina
salt.

▼

Ravioli nudi

Naked ravioli

Preparation time:
30 minutes.
Cooking time:
15 minutes.
2 kg fresh spinach
500 g ricotta
2 eggs
150 g Parmesan
2 tbsp flour
salt
pinch of nutmeg.

Clean and wash the spinach. Cook for ten minutes in a saucepan with just a small amount of boiling, salted water. When cold, squeeze out the excess water and chop finely. Place in a large bowl with the ricotta, eggs, grated parmesan, flour and a pinch of nutmeg. Mix well until all the ingredients are thoroughly blended together. Form the mixture into small pellets, or as Artusi suggests, little croquette-shaped cylinders, about three centimetres in diameter. Coat with flour and leave aside while bringing approximately three litres of water to the boil. Add the salt and drop in the 'naked' ravioli. They are cooked when they rise to the surface. Remove with a strainer and serve immediately in warmed bowls with a sauce. You will need about nine little ravioli per person.

The most suitable sauces for this dish are tomato or sage and butter or Florentine meat sauce.

This variation of ravioli is known as *gnudi* (naked) in Florence and Domenico Romoli gave this name, which is a dialectal corruption of the Renaissance term *ignudi* to his recipe.

▼

Tagliolini alla frantoiana

Tagliolini with oil and herbs

Cut fresh pasta into tagliolini and leave them on the work surface to dry. Finely chop generous quantities of the fresh herbs and leave to soak with the garlic in the oil, which should be freshly pressed, new season's oil. Cook the pasta, drain and toss with the herb dressing. Provide plenty of freshly grated Parmesan or pecorino at the table.

A variation on this recipe is to add a good shake of black pepper and three baby tomatoes, peeled and chopped. In summer time, when there are fresh, juicy tomatoes available, they can be added raw. This variation is in fact a good idea in the summer months, when the new oil, produced in the autumn, is no longer available.

Delicious, newly-pressed olive oil is only to be found for a couple of months. In any case, it will only last for about a year, after which it begins to loose flavour and oxidize, becoming slightly acid and less digestible. So keep an eye

Preparation time:
30 minutes.
Cooking time:
15 minutes.
500 g fresh tagliolini
thyme
rosemary
sage
mint
marjoram
extra-virgin olive oil
2 cloves of garlic
Parmesan or pecorino
salt.
Optional:
three small ripe tomatoes
black pepper.

Crema di porri

Leek soup

Preparation time:
20 minutes.
Cooking time:
30 minutes.
One kg leeks
2 tbsp flour
200 g stock
2 glasses of milk
parsley
Parmesan
salt.

Finely chop the leeks into rings and fry gently in a flameproof earthenware dish. Add the flour and salt, and pour in the stock, stirring all the time. Cook for about twenty minutes, remove from the heat and add the milk. To make the mixture creamy in consistency, you could put it into a blender for a minute or two. Return to the heat for five minutes, add the chopped parsley and grated Parmesan and serve immediately.

Renaissance recipes for this dish suggest adding saffron and cumin to flavour. You could also garnish with a handful of butter-fried croutons.
The flour can be replaced by 300g of potatoes, peeled and finely chopped.
This soup was traditionally served for the San Lorenzo festivities on the 10th August. Historical documents in the Florentine church of San Lorenzo refer to it, also mentioning a savoury flan made with leeks called *porrea*.

Pappa al pomodoro

Bread and tomato soup

Finely chop the onion, leek, carrot, and celery and fry with the oil in a large earthenware pan. Add salt, the peeled and chopped tomatoes, sage and basil and cook for ten minutes. Cut the bread into cubes, add to the tomato mixture and cook, adding water until it becomes smooth and creamy, neither too thick nor too runny. The soup should be served tepid, with olive oil drizzled on top. The flavour can be pepped up with a dash of chili pepper. The forerunner of this dish was called *panunto* or *pancotto* and it contained no vegetables at all. Indeed the original recipe was without tomatoes, as it dates from long before the discovery of America and their arrival in Europe. The ingredients were therefore simply bread, oil, garlic and salt and this tasty, mushy mixture was often used to wean babies.

Preparation time:
25 minutes.
Cooking time:
20 minutes.
one onion
one leek
one carrot
one stick of celery
4 tbsp extra-virgin
olive oil
400 g tomatoes
sprig of fresh sage
basil
6 slices hard
unsalted bread
extra-virgin olive oil
salt
chili pepper.

Pasta e fagioli

Pasta with beans

To soak the beans:
12 hours.
Preparaton time:
15 minutes.
Cooking time:
two hours 20 minutes.
Standing time:
5 minutes.
500 g dried cannellini beans
(one kg if fresh)
sprig fresh sage
5 cloves garlic
rosemary
400 g soup pasta (ditali)
chili pepper
200 g tomatoes
extra-virgin olive oil
salt.

Put the dried cannellini beans in a saucepan with the sage, salt and two cloves of garlic. Cover with water and cook for two hours (one hour if using fresh beans) over a very low heat. Drain two thirds of the beans and mash or blend them. Fry the remaining cloves of garlic and the rosemary; add and lightly toss the raw pasta, stirring continuously. Add a pinch of chili pepper and the mashed beans. Peel and finely chop the tomatoes, add and cook for a couple of minutes then pour in half of the liquid from the beans you have left whole. Allow the pasta to cook, gradually adding the remaining liquid and add more salt if necessary. Lastly, add the whole beans. Remove the rosemary and garlic cloves and leave to stand for five minutes before serving. Remember that half a litre of water is required to cook 100g of dried beans.

Strisce e ceci

Noodles and chick peas

Put the flour in a bowl with a quarter litre of water and a pinch of salt. Work together until you obtain a smooth paste. Form into a ball, place on a work surface and roll out to a thickness of two millimetres. Cut into strips about a centimetre wide and spread out on a clean tea towel. Leave aside.

Lightly fry the cloves of garlic in the oil and add the washed and roughly chopped celery sticks and leaves. Add the peeled and diced tomatoes. Pour half of the cooked chick peas into the fried ingredients with their liquid. Add the pasta noodles and cook, taking care not to let the sauce reduce too much (it might be necessary to add a little boiling water). In the meantime, mash the remaining chick peas and add to the pasta. Remove the garlic and the celery and serve with chili pepper, black pepper and oil. For a different flavour, replace the celery with rosemary.

To soak the chick peas:
12 hours.
Preparation time:
40 minutes.
Cooking time:
two hours 30 minutes.
For the pasta:
300 g plain flour
salt.
For the sauce:
2 cloves of garlic
2 tbsp extra-virgin
olive oil
four sticks of green celery
(or a sprig of rosemary)
3 small ripe tomatoes
300 g chick peas
black pepper
chili pepper
salt.

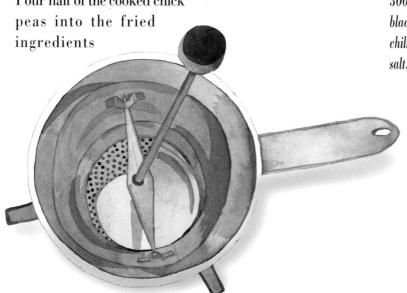

▼

Ribollita

Vegetable and bread soup

Preparation time:
20 minutes.
Cooking time:
one hour 45 minutes.
300 g potatoes
300 g savoy cabbage
300 g black cabbage (kale)
4 ripe tomatoes
500 g fresh
cannellini beans
(250 g if dried)
200 g Swiss chard
one red onion
3 cloves garlic
2 sticks celery
2 carrots
2 courgettes
thyme
4 tbsp extra-virgin
olive oil
wholemeal bread, a day or
two old
chili pepper
salt.

It is best to cook the beans on their own first, perhaps the day before, as they cook much more slowly than the rest of the vegetables (see the recipe for *fagioli in olio*). Clean, wash, peel and chop all the vegetables and put into a large saucepan. Cover with water and cook for 40 minutes. Remove from the heat and add the cooked beans. Fry the onion with the oil and chili pepper (if liked) in an earthenware casserole; add the thyme leaves. Cut the bread into cubes and put into the casserole; now pour in the soup and cook gently for about ten minutes, then leave to stand off the heat. Before serving, it should be put in the oven to cook again for twenty minutes, with olive oil drizzled on top. You can also garnish the soup with rings of raw onion before putting it into the oven as, once baked, they give a really special flavour to this favourite classic.

Fette col cavolo nero

Cabbage crostini

Clean and wash the cabbage (or kale) carefully and cook in a litre and a half of boiling, salted water. When it is cooked, toast the bread, rub a clove of garlic over each slice and place in soup bowls. Pour over a little of the cooking water to moisten and top with the cabbage leaves, roughly chopped.

Pour over the oil and dust with freshly ground black pepper.

Green vegetables have always been a great favourite with Florentines. During the 14th century boiled green vegetables on slices of toasted bread were sold from hot food stands in the city. This tradition has disappeared, but to savour the original smells and flavours, you need only visit San Ambrogio and San Lorenzo markets.

Preparation time:
20 minutes.
Cooking time:
one hour.
one kg black cabbage (kale)
12 slices of bread
garlic
extra-virgin olive oil
black pepper
salt.

▼

Brodo

Meat broth

*Preparation time:
15 minutes.
Cooking time:
one hour 30 minutes.
500 g beef (lean)
half a chicken
one carrot
one stick of celery
one onion
three ripe tomatoes
parsley
salt.*

Cut the beef and chicken (with the skin removed) into pieces. Put into a large saucepan with the peeled and chopped vegetables. Add two litres of cold water, the salt and parsley, tied into a bunch. Cook very slowly for an hour and a half. Remove the meat and strain the soup. If you wish to remove all the grease, it should be left to cool completely first. Beef soup has always been considered an excellent tonic for building up one's strength and energy. Repeating a common, though quite incorrect belief, Pellegrino Artusi recommended it for upset stomachs. Solid foods provide a better cure, however. Try supping it on a cold, winter's evening, garnished with chopped parsley, or with del-

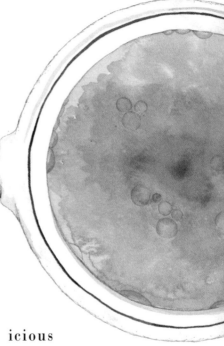

icious taglierini made from fresh pasta. Bartolomeo Sacchi suggested, "One could add spices to this soup, as long as it is not intended for invalids. This is good sustenance for the elderly and ailing".

Stracciatella

Egg soup

Peel and grind the almonds, beat the eggs, grate the Parmesan and crumble the bread. Mix all together in a bowl and taste for salt. Bring the beef stock to the boil and pour in the egg mixture. Cook for two minutes, beating with a whisk all the time. Serve very hot, garnished with freshly chopped parsley.

Bartolomeo Sacchi's recipe began, "Mix together seven eggs, half a pound of grated cheese and breadcrumbs...", while Maestro Martino's name for it was *zanzarelli*. For Pellegrino Artusi it was *panata* (bread soup) and he suggested adding cooked peas or green vegetables to it, mixing them in and heating through well just before serving.

In my family this soup is traditionally served at lunch on Easter Sunday.

Preparation time:
20 minutes.
Cooking time:
one hour 40 minutes.
1.5 litre stock
200 g Parmesan
100 g bread
100 g almonds
3 eggs
parsley
salt.

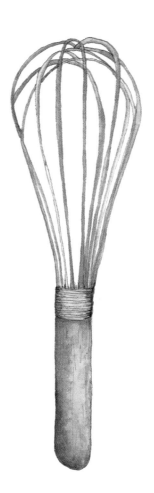

▼

Penne strascicate

'Scrambled' pasta

Preparation time:
20 minutes.
Cooking time:
One hour.
500 g penne
300 g Florentine
meat sauce
extra-virgin olive oil
Parmesan
salt
black pepper.

Cook the penne in boiling, salted water until just 'al dente'. Pour the meat sauce into a large heavy iron frying pan (this dish is best using the thicker sauce cooked for one hour). Add the penne, pour over the olive oil and toss and stir over a high flame for about five minutes. Do not allow the sauce to stick to the pan, and mix the pasta in thoroughly. Grate a good helping of Parmesan and stir in off the heat. When serving, offer freshly ground black pepper.

As an alternative to the meat sauce, you could use the liquid from a good stew.

Remember you need a litre of water to every hundred grams of pasta. Salt the water when it comes to the boil and since this will lower the temperature, wait a few seconds until it boils again before adding the pasta.

The feast of San Lorenzo is on the 10th of August and celebrations are held in the area around the church. Traditionally lasagne with meat sauce was served to the townsfolk who came to enjoy the festivities. The custom still continues today and large slices of refreshing watermelon are served to all afterwards.

Penne trippate alla fiorentina

Penne with Florentine-style tripe

Prepare the tripe following the recipe on page 60.

Cook the penne in boiling water until *al dente*. Chop the tripe into small cubes and toss in a frying pan with the drained pasta. Before serving, garnish with a generous helping of grated Parmesan, or sprinkle it over the pasta and grill in the oven for a few minutes. Tripe is a typically Florentine dish and stalls selling cooked tripe are a traditional feature of the city. Several still exist in the city centre (there is even one quite near to Piazza della Signoria) and the unusual, sweet aroma they produce is quite unfamiliar to most visitors. These tripe-sellers not only provide a tasty, hot snack, but also sell the raw tripe for this pasta dish.

Tripe stalls have existed in Florence since the fourteenth century: then the tripe was served on a slice of bread moistened with stock. The custom still exists, though today the tripe is served, rather more conveniently, inside a bread roll.

Preparation time:
30 minutes.
Cooking time:
45 minutes.
500 g penne (large and without grooves)
300 g tripe
Parmesan
salt.

▼

Pappardelle sulla lepre

Pappardelle with hare sauce

Preparation time:
40 minutes.
Cooking time:
two hours.
One carrot
one onion
one stick of celery
4 tbsp extra-virgin
olive oil
parsley
2 kg hare (or rabbit)
500 g fresh pasta
one glass red wine
2 tomatoes
one lemon
Parmesan
salt.

Wash, peel and finely chop the carrot, onion, celery, and parsley. Fry over a medium heat in a large pan. Cut the cleaned hare into large pieces and add to the vegetables. Increase the heat and brown on all sides; add the glass of wine and let it evaporate rapidly.

When the hare is well cooked, remove it from the pan, bone then chop the meat and return it to the rest of the sauce. Add a glass of warm water and the peeled, chopped tomatoes and salt. Cook over a low heat for ten minutes.

If liked, add some grated lemon rind, though be careful to avoid the pith, as this lends a bitter flavour to the meat.

Cut fresh pasta into broad strips (pappardelle) and cook in boiling, salted water. When cooked, drain and tip into the pan on top of the sauce. Toss gently for a minute and serve, topped with grated Parmesan, in a large bowl, warmed with some of the pasta water.

Domenico Romoli wrote: "Hare with

▼

papardelle...use fine, soft lasagne to line the bowls and pour the meat sauce on top, flavoured with pepper".

Pellegrino Artusi suggested adding "a pinch of nutmeg", but added, "I think it enhances the flavour, but if you don't like it then don't bother".

In Florence, the pappardelle are traditionally placed on top of the sauce and then gently mixed through and not vice versa, as this method tends to spoil the subtlety of the flavours.

▼

Panzanella

Bread salad

To soak the bread:
30 minutes.
Preparation time:
20 minutes.
Standing time:
one hour.
12 slices of bread
100 g green chicory
50 g rocket leaves
50 g endive
one spring onion
basil leaves
extra virgin olive oil

The success of this extremely simple recipe depends on two things: the bread must be unsalted, country bread, a day or two old, and the rest of the ingredients must be top quality and fresh.
Leave the slices of bread to soak in cold water for half an hour. Clean the salad and vegetables and chop finely. Place in a salad bowl and add the fresh basil leaves.

Using your hands, squeeze the bread thoroughly to remove the water and reduce to breadcrumbs. Add to the vegetables in the bowl and dress with oil, salt and vinegar. Toss well and leave in the fridge for an hour before serving.

There are several variations of this recipe, all of which add various other vegetables, but to me these seem a travesty of the real panzanella. You could, however, add cucumber and/or tomatoes, chopped or finely sliced, and a shake of pepper.

Choose the wine to accompany this dish with care as the vinegar will affect its flavour. In the past it was eaten with a weak, watery wine called *vinello* or *acquerello*, made by soaking the bunches of grapes left after the wine pressing in water and then squeezing them out. A light, young red wine is therefore best.

salt
wine vinegar.
Optional:
two salad tomatoes
cucumber
black pepper.

CUTS OF MEAT

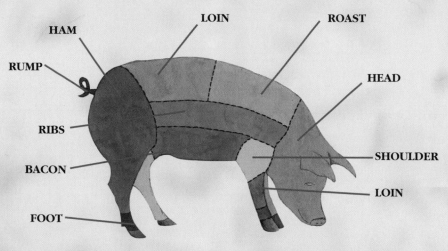

HAM
RUMP
LOIN
ROAST
HEAD
RIBS
BACON
SHOULDER
LOIN
FOOT

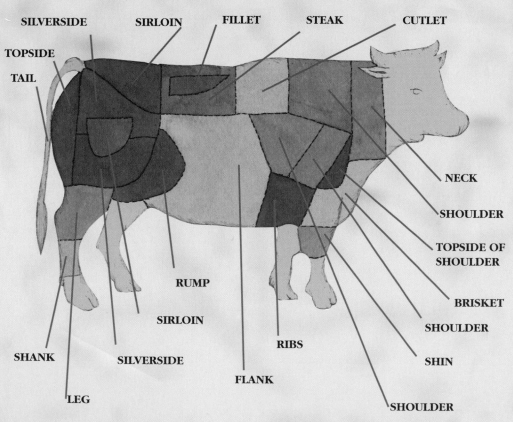

SILVERSIDE
TOPSIDE
TAIL
SIRLOIN
FILLET
STEAK
CUTLET
NECK
SHOULDER
TOPSIDE OF SHOULDER
BRISKET
SHOULDER
SHIN
SHANK
SILVERSIDE
RUMP
SIRLOIN
RIBS
FLANK
LEG
SHOULDER

Piatti di mezzo

Main courses

▼

Valigette

Beef rolls

Layer onto each fillet of steak a piece of ham, a slice of cheese, a segment of artichoke, some parsley and a pinch of salt.

Roll the meat up to form a neat roulade and tie with a piece of string or close firmly with a toothpick.

Chop and dice the carrots, artichoke stems and leaves, if any are left over; fry in the oil until soft in a large casserole. Add the beef roulades and brown on all sides. Dissolve a pinch of salt in the glass of wine and pour over the meat; allow to evaporate rapidly and continue to cook over a low heat for forty minutes. If the gravy has dried out during the cooking, remove the meat, add some more wine and a drop of oil and leave on the heat to reduce slightly. Remove the string or the toothpicks before serving, as it is rather unpleasant to find yourself munching on them! Fried or puréed potatoes are the perfect accompaniment for this dish.

Domenico Romoli called them "stuffed, stewed parcels", however, his recipe contained some quite different ingredients, while Pellegrino Artusi refers to "artichoke-stuffed steaks".

Preparation time:
20 minutes.
Cooking time:
45 minutes.
900 g thin slices
silverside steak
150 g cooked ham
150 g Fontina cheese,
thinly sliced
parsley
3 carrots
5 artichokes
4 tbsp extra-virgin
olive oil
one glass white wine
salt.

▼

Trippa alla fiorentina

Florentine-style tripe

*Preparation time:
30 minutes.
Cooking time:
40 minutes.
1.5 kg tripe, blanched
and boiled
one onion
one carrot
one stick of celery
30 g butter
2 tbsp extra-virgin
olive oil
500 g tomatoes
Parmesan
salt.*

Using only the best parts of the tripe, either the meatier part or the spongy, honeycomb part, cut it into very thin strips. Clean, wash and chop the onion, carrot and celery and put into an earthenware or metal pan with the butter. Fry well and add the oil and tripe. When golden in colour, add the tomatoes, peeled and chopped very finely. Add salt and cook over a very low heat for about half an hour, until the sauce has reduced almost completely, stirring frequently to prevent sticking. The tripe may be served immediately without any garnish, or alternatively sprinkle some grated Parmesan over and brown in the oven for five minutes. Tripe is best served with boiled or puréed potatoes or, if preferred, with cannellini beans in oil.

Bartolomeo Sacchi took his recipe from Maestro Martino, "A main course of tripe…when cooked and served on the plates, sprinkle well with ground spices. Some also add grated cheese".

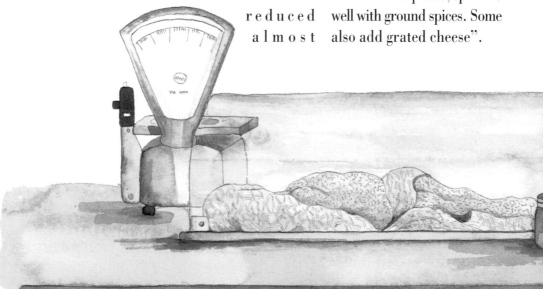

Trippa a insalata

Tripe salad

As for the previous recipe, buy ready prepared tripe. Fill a large saucepan with water, bring to the boil and slide in the tripe. Cook for about half an hour and add salt.

Drain the tripe well and allow to cool. Cut into rectangular strips about one centimetre by four. Put into a large salad bowl and dress with oil, salt, pepper (if desired) and a few drops of vinegar. Add the finely chopped parsley, carrot, celery and peeled and diced tomatoes. Leave in the fridge for an hour so that the flavours can mingle.

You could also serve this dish as an antipasto (using only half a kilo of tripe) or as a quick, one-course lunch. This and the previous recipe are seasonal variations on a really quite delicious food; while the salad is perfect for the spring or summer months, the *trippa alla fiorentina* is more suitable in cold winter weather.

Preparation time:
20 minutes.
Cooking time:
30 minutes.
Refrigeration time:
one hour.
One kg tripe
parsley
green celery
one carrot
salad tomatoes
salt
black pepper
extra-virgin olive oil
vinegar.

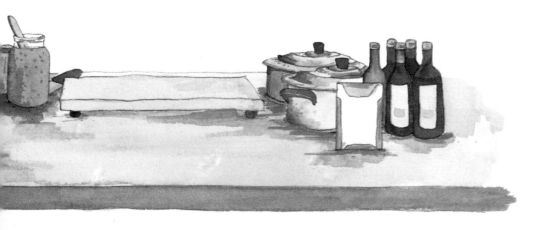

▼

Uova frittellate o affrittellate

Fried eggs

Preparation time:
5 minutes.
Cooking time:
5 minutes.
12 fresh eggs
5 tbsp extra-virgin
olive oil
bread
salt
black pepper.

Put the oil into the frying pan and heat slightly. Break in the eggs, or as Pellegrino Artusi said "drip" them directly into the pan, taking care not to break the yolks. Cook very slowly, tilting the pan so that the hot oil runs over the yolks. When the whites have become opaque, quickly salt the eggs and remove from the heat. You could also grind some black pepper on top, if liked or cook the eggs with finely sliced bacon. Fry the rashers rapidly in very hot oil so they become crispy, and then place the eggs on top.

It is most important to serve the right kind of bread with this dish - it should be as fresh as possible with a crispy crust. Maestro Martino called these *Ova frictellate*, while for Bartolomeo Sacchi, they were

'Florentine-style eggs'. Pellegrino Artusi suggested "If you wish to have a sauce on them, you could try tomatoes...I have also seen them served on top of a layer of potato puré, about a centimetre thick, or over spinach tossed in butter".

Frittata di carciofi (tortino)

Artichoke omlette (artichoke pie)

Carefully clean the artichokes until you obtain a good sized heart. Cut each one into about six slices. Put into a large frying pan with oil and cook over a low heat. Use a fork to check when they are soft and well cooked (about fifteen minutes), increase the heat and pour in the beaten eggs and chopped parsley. Fry for about thirty seconds then begin to gently shake the saucepan, holding it just slightly above the flame. When the omlette slides freely without sticking in the pan, flip it over onto the other side or slide it on to a plate and then back into the pan. Continue to gently shake the pan as before and when completely cooked, put the omlette on a large dish and serve hot, garnished with segments of lemon. This is almost like a pie, and can, in fact, also be cooked in the oven, but use a quiche dish in this case. Other fillings, such as courgettes, onions or potatoes can be used but only the artichoke omlette is served with lemon.

Pellegrino Artusi wrote of these 'artichokes in a pan', "In Tuscany, this is considered to be a good, solid and inexpensive family meal. It can be served at lunch, either as a starter or as a main course".

Preparation time:
15 minutes.
Cooking time:
15 minutes.
9 medium sized artichokes
6 eggs
extra-virgin olive oil
salt
parsley.
To garnish:
one lemon.

▼

Stracotto

Braised beef

Preparation time:
20 minutes.
Cooking time:
two hours 30 minutes.
1.5 kg beef (shoulder, brisket
chuck or stewing)
5 tbsp extra-virgin
olive oil
one onion
2 carrots
2 sticks of celery
one garlic clove
one glass red wine
500 g tomatoes
parsley
salt.

Tie the joint of beef firmly and brown well in a saucepan with high sides. Chop or slice the onion, carrot and celery and add to the meat with the clove of garlic. Sauté for ten minutes. Increase the heat, add the glass of wine and allow to evaporate, taste for salt and add the peeled tomatoes. Lower the flame and cook gently for two hours with the lid on the pan. Before removing from the heat, add the roughly chopped parsley. If, at the end of the cooking time, the sauce seems a bit too liquid, increase the heat for a couple of minutes, add a drop of oil and allow to reduce. Cut the beef joint into slices and arrange on a warmed serving dish. For a smoother sauce, put in the blender briefly, reheat and then pour it over the sliced meat. Serve immediately. The name of this recipe act-ually means 'overcooked', but in fact it is a good description, as it is intended for the tougher, tasty cuts of meat which require long, slow cooking.

Before the discovery of America and t h e importation of tomatoes, *stracotto* was cooked with *agresto* - a sauce made from crushed, tart grapes, boiled and flavoured with c l o v e s , cinnamon and the juice of squeezed onions.

Roventini

Pig's blood fritters

One litre of pig's blood will make about thirty fritters. Sift the flour over the blood, add the egg yolks and whisk together thoroughly to eliminate lumps. Oil a small, cast iron frying pan and pour in a ladleful of the mixture at a time. As soon as the mixture becomes firm, turn as with an omlette or pancake.

Serve very hot with grated Parmesan sprinkled on top and eat with a thick slice of wholemeal bread.
Romoli's advice for this recipe is: "...take a flat plate, put fresh, green bay leaves on it, put the black pudding on top, then sprinkle with pepper and white salt (from Volterra). Above all, eat while still very hot".

Preparation time:
10 minutes.
Cooking time:
15 minutes.
one litre fresh
pig's blood
2 tbsp plain white flour
2 egg yolks
Parmesan
extra-virgin olive oil
salt
bread.

▼

Lesso

Boiled meats

Preparation time:
15 minutes.
Cooking time:
one hour 30 minutes.
1.5 kg assorted cuts of beef
(shin, silverside, rump)
2 litres water
one onion
one stick of celery
one carrot
salt.
Optional:
half a calf's tongue,
fresh or corned.

Bring the water to the boil, add salt, the onion, celery, and carrot.

Put the meats into the water and cook slowly for an hour and a half.

Remove, place on a warm platter and serve hot with green sauce (page 14) and vegetables preserved in oil. You could also include, along with the various cuts of beef, half a calf's tongue, either fresh or corned (corned tongue is a Florentine speciality).

It is also excellent when cold, with green sauce. If using tongue, remember to peel it once it has been boiled.

If any of the meat is left over, you can use it to make excellent rissoles for frying (see *Polpettone e polpette*) and if you like onions, you could also make the traditional dish, known in Florence as *francesina*. Here is the recipe for about half a kilo of meat:

Peel three or four medium-sized red onions and cut into thick rings.

Put in a saucepan with a clove of garlic and four tablespoons of oil. Heat through, cover and cook over a low flame for about twenty minutes, stirring occasionally with a wooden spoon. Slice the boiled meat about half a centimetre thick and place in the frying pan; increase the heat and combine well, stirring and turning with the spoon; cook for a couple of minutes.

Dissolve a few drops of tomato concentrate in a glass of hot water and add to the meat with the salt and pepper. Cook uncovered until the sauce has reduced; serve hot.

Apicius had a different recipe to accompany boiled meat:

"White sauce. Pepper, *garum*, wine, rue, onion, pine nuts, wine with salt, pepper and spices, a few pieces of moistened bread, oil. When the meat is cooked, spread this sauce over it".

Garum was a sauce made from fish and was a basic ingredient in Roman cooking: used in drops, it often replaced salt.

▼

Fegato alla salvia

Liver with sage

Preparation time:
10 minutes.
Cooking time:
5 minutes.
12 slices of calf's liver cut
about half a centimetre thick
(approx. 900 g)
5 cloves of garlic
5 tbsp extra-virgin
olive oil
flour
fresh sage leaves
salt.

Remove the thin skin tissue around the slices of liver, to prevent them shrivelling while cooking. Coat both sides with flour.

Using a large frying pan, gently fry the cloves of garlic in the oil; add the washed and dried sage leaves and when the oil begins to sizzle slide in the slices of liver. Fry on each side for a couple of minutes so that the outside is crisp and golden but inside the liver remains soft and tender. Salt both sides, remove from the frying pan and place on a platter lined with kitchen paper to drain off the excess oil. Before bringing to the table, remove the kitchen paper and any remaining leaves of sage. If you prefer some sauce with the meat, pour a glass of white wine over the liver and let it reduce well, arrange on a large platter and bring to the table with the pepper mill for those who like. With or without a sauce, liver is delicious with fried potatoes or a fresh salad.

▼

Fegatelli

Liver skewers

Cut the liver into large cubes (about 3 cm square). Soak the stomach lining and then cut into 10 cm squares. Wrap each piece of liver with the lining. Thread on to a steel skewer, alternating with a bay leaf and a cube of bread. Roast on a spit over a wood fire or in the oven, or put in a rectangular aluminium pan and brown well on all sides, turning occasionally. Cook until the liver is tender, testing with a wooden toothpick. The pieces of liver could also be alternated with diced chicken or turkey breast, or pork loin and sausages.

Apicius wrote: "Wrap with the lining of the stomach and roast on a gridiron: serve". Bartolomeo Sacchi suggested, "Take some pig's liver...sprinkle with salt, fennel seeds, and powdered, sweet spices...".

Preparation time:
30 minutes.
Cooking time:
30 minutes.
900 g pig's liver
a piece of stomach lining
bay leaves
bread
salt.

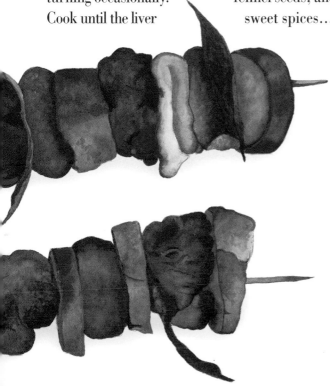

Polpettone e polpette

Meat loaf and rissoles

*Preparation time:
30 minutes.
Cooking time:
40 minutes.
400 g minced meat
100 g prosciutto
one egg
salt
parsley
one slice of bread
milk*

Soak the bread in warm milk, then squeeze it dry and reduce to crumbs. Mix together with the minced meat, chopped ham, egg, salt and chopped parsley. Add the grated Parmesan.
Blend together thoroughly for a few minutes, then, with your hands slightly moistened, form into an oval

shaped 'loaf'. Be very careful not to leave any cracks or gaps, otherwise the loaf will open and fall apart during the cooking. Pour the oil into a large, earthenware dish with low sides and warm gently. Roll the meat loaf lightly in the flour and place in the dish. Brown evenly all over so that the surface forms a

To make rissoles instead, roll the mixture into small rounds and fry them gently in oil until cooked; add a glass of white wine and let it evaporate. Sprinkle with chopped parsley and serve. This recipe was used by Apicius, Maestro Martino and Bartolomeo Sacchi, who wrote, "This dish is commonly known as *mortadella*…it is good for both the heart and liver". Domenico Romoli calls them *tomaselle*.

At the banquet to celebrate the christening of Cosimo I in 1519 a dish similar to meat loaf was served, though with the slightly more pompous title of "pie of veal minced like a loaf". Don't forget that meat loaf and rissoles can also be made from any left over boiled meat, diced very finely using a large chopping knife.

crispy crust. Add the chop ped carrot, celery and onion, toss until golden and pour in half a glass of white wine. Leave to evaporate and add half a glass of water. It takes approximately half an hour for the loaf to cook, but it should be frequently checked to prevent it sticking to the pan.

Leave it to set for a few minutes and then cut into thick slices. Pour its own hot gravy over and serve with potato purée. Add some sliced mushrooms to the sauce for a really special flavour.

100 g Parmesan
plain flour
3 tbsp extra-virgin olive oil
one carrot
one stick of celery
one onion
one glass white wine.

▼

Stufato

Stew

Preparation time:
15 minutes.
Cooking time:
2 hours.
one kg beef
(silverside, chuck, or
stewing steak)
4 tbsp extra-virgin
olive oil
4 cloves garlic
one glass white wine
parsley
salt.

Cut the meat into cubes. Heat the oil in an aluminium pan over a medium heat. When it begins to smoke, add the meat and brown well on all sides, stirring briskly with a wooden spoon so that it doesn't stick.

Now add the whole garlic cloves and when they become golden, add the wine and let it evaporate rapidly. Add salt, lower the flame and leave to cook slowly covered for two hours until the meat is very tender and a smooth, thick sauce has formed.

If the sauce reduces too much during the cooking time, add half a glass of water or watered-down wine.

Serve hot, sprinkled with chopped parsley. In the autumn, when fresh, porcini mushrooms are available, you could add some slices to the sauce for a special flavour. The stew is also excellent with peas added to the meat about twenty minutes before the end of the cooking time. Another alternative is to add peeled and roughly diced potatoes, but these require and extra half hour to forty minutes to cook.

▼

Peposo

Peppery stew

Put the garlic, oil, wine, steak cut into cubes, salt and freshly ground pepper (at least a level soup spoon) into a large earthenware dish. Cover completely with cold water, put on the lid and place in the oven, previously heated to 180° C. Cook for about two hours, checking that it does not dry out too much; if so, add a little warm water. The meat should be very tender by the end and the sauce well reduced and thick.

Peeled and diced tomatoes may be added to flavour the sauce. Legend has it that Filippo Brunelleschi often ate this sauce when the dome of the cathedral was being built. Indeed the recipe is also known as 'kiln stew' because the meat was cooked in the furnace along with the bricks. Brunelleschi had his own furnace on the building site so that he could check every single phase in the making of his masterpiece. Thus his *peposo* stew was baked alongside the very bricks used to build this unique structure.

Preparation time:
20 minutes.
Cooking time:
2 hours.
1 kg chuck steak
6 cloves of garlic
3 tbsp extra-virgin olive oil
one glass red wine
salt
black pepper.

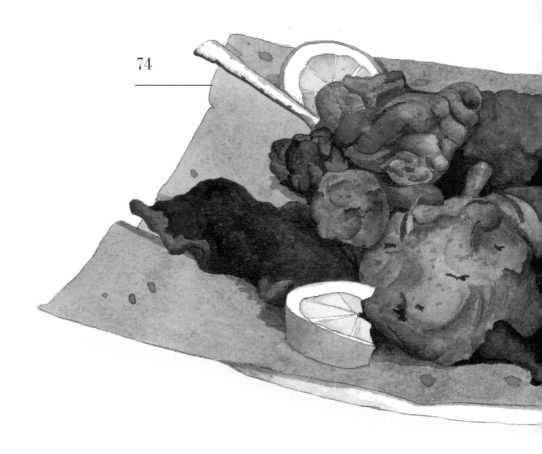

Fritto

Mixed fried meats

Preparation time:
30 minutes.
Cooking time:
20 minutes.
800 g meat
plain flour
2 eggs
breadcrumbs
extra-virgin olive oil
salt.

For a really delicious meal you will need a good assortment of various meats such as chicken, turkey, rabbit, lamb and calf's brains.

The chicken should be fried skinless and the brains should be plunged in boiling water for a few minutes and the membrane then carefully removed. Cut all the meats into small pieces and toss in the flour. Dip each piece into the beaten, salted eggs.

The ribs of lamb and the turkey breast should be dipped first in the egg and then in the breadcrumbs. Drop the pieces into a generous amount of hot oil and fry gently on all sides

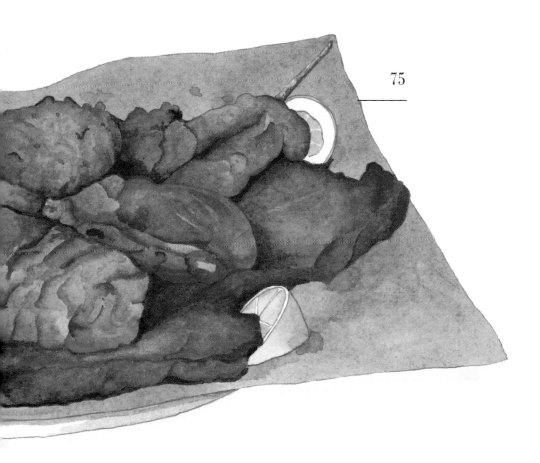

for ten minutes. Increase the heat until they turn golden brown. Drain all the meats on kitchen paper and salt well before serving. Garnish with lemon quarters.

Fresh, mixed green salad goes well with this fry. In the past, lard or animal fat, both of which are much heavier than olive oil, were used for frying. Our ancestors must have been made of sterner stuff than us however, for Bartolomeo Sacchi, after admitting that the *fritto* was "a dish that is difficult to digest", went on to praise it, claiming that "it stifles bile and is good for the heart, liver and kidneys".

▼

Bistecca

T-bone steak

Preparation time:
15 minutes.
Cooking time:
10 minutes, each steak.
2 top quality
T-bone steaks each
weighing between 800 g-1 kg
extra-virgin olive oil
salt
pepper.

It is one of the oddities of language that in English beefsteak means a fillet without a bone, and this has become a common acceptance in many regions of Italy. In Florence, however, a fillet is called a bracciola, while a steak (bistecca) is a large entrecote, including the fillet. This recipe is exclusively for those who like their meat rare: a Florentine steak which is well cooked is not just a waste, it is a total heresy. The inside of the steak must be tender and succulent, while the outside must be crisp and have a well-grilled appearance. The steaks should be about five centimetres thick, tender and of the very best quality. Prepare a cast-iron roasting dish (or much better, if possible, a gridiron over coals) and heat it well.

Cook the beef on this for five minutes on each side. Do not pierce the meat with a fork and use a wooden palette to turn it over. Meanwhile, warm the plates so that the meat does not get cold immediately as it would loose much of its flavour. Salt,

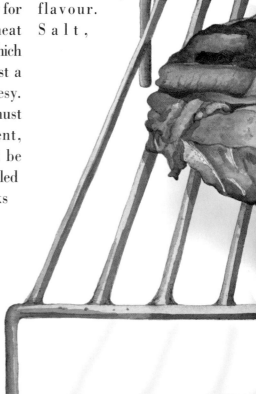

▼

pepper and oil should be added after serving. A word of advice - or rather, an order! Never add salt while the meat is cooking. This draws out the juices and the moisture then prevents it becoming browned and crispy on the outside, remaining 'slack' and fleshy instead. Fried potatoes and salad are the best accompaniment, but you could also serve freshly cooked beans in oil.

If you have the misfortune to be abstemious, then you should drink only natural mineral water with the steak. But if, as I hope, you enjoy a good wine, then a vintage Chianti classico produced around Florence or Siena is ideal.

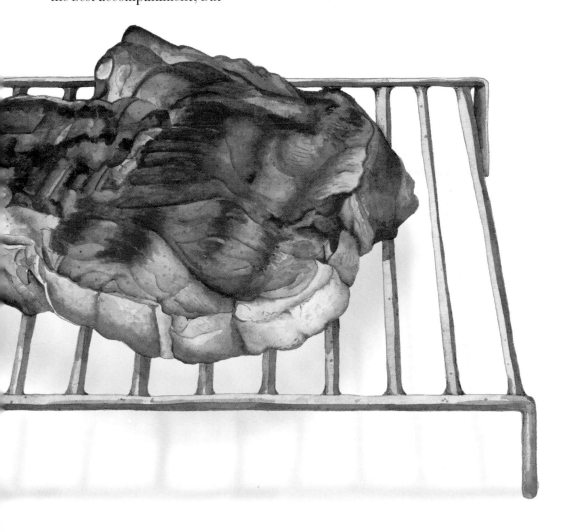

▼

Arista

Roast loin of pork

*Preparation time:
10 minutes.
Cooking time:
two hours.
2 kg loin of pork
sage
rosemary
garlic
white wine
salt
extra-virgin olive oil.*

Ask your butcher to cut the meat away from the ribs, but leave it attached to the main bone. Rub salt and oil into the surface, place in a roasting dish and put in the oven, preheated to 180° C. Cook slowly for two hours, basting and turning frequently, so that it becomes evenly golden brown on all sides. Remove from the oven and cut the meat away from the bone. Serve sliced, with a gravy made from the sage, rosemary, and garlic, fried together lightly; drench with wine and let it evaporate.

The roast can also be eaten cold in the summertime: slice the pork very thinly, arrange on a large platter, heat the gravy and pour over just before serving. However, it can also be served without any gravy or juices. With the warm roast pork, salad and roast or puréed potatoes, cannellini beans, or spinach sautéed in butter are best, while cold roast pork is delicious with a crisp salad, fresh beans in oil, or pinzimonio.

Artusi claimed that the name arista was derived from the Greek exclamation *ariste* (good), uttered, apparantly, by an orthodox bishop on first tasting the dish during the Council of Florence between the Roman and Greek churches in 1430. However, the name comes from the Latin *arista* (a spike, or spine, referring to the jagged bone in this cut of meat).

Moreover, the word is also found in a story by Sacchetti, written before the Council of Florence.

▼

Bistecchine di maiale

Pork chops

The term bistecca in pork butchery refers to chops in Florence and not the fillet as in other regions.

Put the chops in an ovenproof dish, scatter the finely chopped herbs on top and pour over the oil and a little water. Cook in the oven at 180°C until the water has been completely absorbed. Turn on the grill and cook the chops on both sides until golden brown. Sprinkle with salt and serve with beans in oil or a salad.

In traditional Florentine cookery, pork is one of the most frequently-used meats and consequently many recipes exist for both fresh and cured pork. In the countryside, on farms and villages, the killing and dressing of the pig, which usually took place in late autumn, in November or December, was always an important event in the seasonal calendar. Friends and neighbours were invited to celebrate at a large lunch and roast pork ribs and roventini (see page 65) were served.

Preparation time:
10 minutes.
Cooking time:
40 minutes.
2 kg pork chops
about 2 cm thick
thyme
marjoram
sage
rosemary
fennel seeds
2 tbsp extra-virgin
olive oil.

▼

Rosticciana

Pork ribs

*Preparation time:
10 minutes.
Cooking time:
one hour.
2 kg pork ribs
rosemary
garlic
one glass white wine
salt.*

The term *rosticciana* or *rostinciana* refers to pork ribs in Florence.

Cut the ribs into sections about three centimetres thick. Put in a large frying pan and add the rosemary, garlic and a glass of water. Cover and cook over a low heat for about an hour, turning frequently, until the water has completely evaporated. Increase the heat, add the salt and wine and allow to reduce gradually, browning the meat evenly on all sides. The ribs can also be roasted in the oven: put all the ingredients together in a rectangular, aluminium oven dish and roast for forty minutes at 180° C. If you have a charcoal or wood fire, or barbecue, you can cook them on a warmed gridiron for about an hour until golden. Sprinkle with salt before bringing to the table and serve with beans in oil or sautéed spinach.

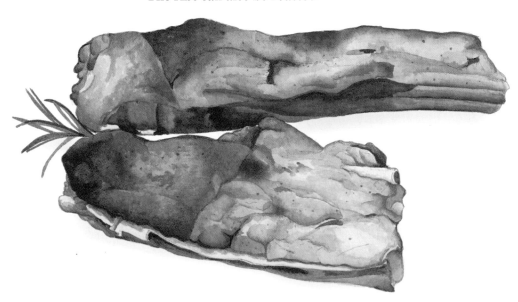

Salsicce

Italian pork sausage

Separate the sausages and pierce with a toothpick. Cook in a little boiling water for five minutes to remove some of the excess fat. Drain and put in a frying pan over a high flame.

Fry in their own fat until they become golden brown all over, taste for salt and serve with fagioli all'uccelletto (white beans in tomatoes - page 95) or sautéed spinach. The sausages can also be added to the vegetables and cooked together with them for a few minutes before bringing to the table.

Sellers of dressed and cured pork (including salsicce), dried fish and cheeses are known as *pizzicagnoli* in Florence and their shop windows are extremely enticing, filled with delicious, mouth-watering produce.

Preparation time:
10 minutes.
Cooking time:
15 minutes.
10 fresh Italian pork sausages
salt.

▼

Coniglio ripieno

Stuffed rabbit

Preparation time:
20 minutes.
Cooking time:
45 minutes.
One rabbit, about 2 kg in
weight
2 slices cooked ham
or streaky bacon
parsley
150 g Fontina cheese
4 artichokes
one carrot
one spring onion
one stick of celery
4 tbsp extra-virgin
olive oil
2 glasses white wine
salt.

Ask your butcher to bone the rabbit. Lay it out flat, boned side up, sprinkle with salt and layer it with the ham or bacon, parsley leaves, thin slices of Fontina, three of the artichokes, cleaned and cut into slices. Roll the meat up widthwise (from tail to head) and tie with string. Put in an ovenproof dish and fry gently over a medium heat. Roughly chop the carrot, spring onion, celery and remaining artichoke. Add to the rabbit and soften the vegetables for a few minutes. Pour in the wine, cover and cook for thirty minutes. If the wine was insufficient to prevent the rabbit sticking to the pan, then add a little warm water. Brown the meat on all sides under a medium grill, turning occasionally. Remove and allow to cool slightly before cutting into fairly thin slices. For a smooth sauce, put it in the blender briefly, then reheat and pour over the slices of rabbit arranged on a warmed serving dish.

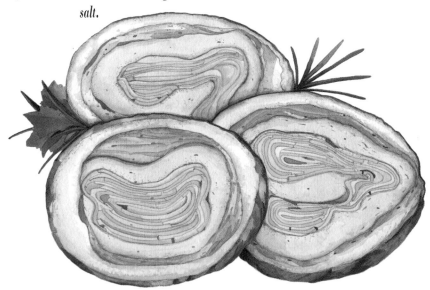

Pesci

Fish

Baccalà

Dried cod

Wash and clean the leeks, chop into thin rings, put in a frying pan with the warmed oil and cook gently. Rinse the dried cod, cut into medium-sized chunks, coat with flour and add to the leeks. Brown the fish on all sides, taking care not to let it stick to the pan. Add the peeled and chopped tomatoes and cook over a low heat for twenty minutes. Sprinkle with chopped parsley and a good pinch of freshly ground black pepper, if liked.

Usually you should not need to add salt to dried cod, but do taste it to check before removing from the heat.

Cod is fished in the Arctic or Antarctic and is known either as baccalà or stoccafisso. Baccalà is preserved by salting and has to be soaked for four days to remove the excess salt, while stoccafisso is dried in the open air and has to be soaked for fifteen days then pounded and flaked.

Preparation time:
15 minutes.
Cooking time:
25 minutes.
1.2 kg dried cod
already soaked
3 leeks
5 tbsp extra-virgin
olive oil
plain white flour
500 g ripe tomatoes
parsley.

▼

Calamari in zimino

Stewed squid

Preparation time:
30 minutes.
Cooking time:
30 minutes.
1.2 kg of
medium-sized squid
1.5 kg Swiss chard or spinach
5 tbsp extra-virgin
olive oil
3 cloves garlic
500 g tomatoes
salt.

Clean, wash and cook the chard or spinach. Clean the squid, removing the contents of the sac, or buy them ready-prepared. Chop the sac into rings about one centimetre thick. Put in a pan or casserole with the oil and garlic and leave to absorb the flavours. Squeeze the liquid out of the the vegetables and chop. Add to the squid and heat through with the peeled and diced tomatoes and a pinch of salt. Cook over a medium heat for twenty minutes. Remove the garlic cloves and serve the squid hot on a warmed serving dish. Alternatively, the whole dish could be cooked in an earthenware casserole and brought straight to the table. This is one of the most characteristic Florentine fish dishes, but Artusi, who was from the Romagna, clearly was not enthusiastic about it, grumbling that, "The Florentines in particular, are so keen on green vegetables that they put them in absolutely everything. Consequently they add chards to this dish, which is about as suitable as soup at Holy

Sogliola alla fiorentina

Florentine-style sole

Melt half the butter in a casserole and add the fillets of sole, coated with flour. Fry on both sides until golden and add the wine; allow to evaporate. Wash, boil, chop and 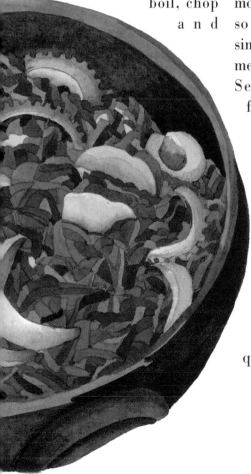 toss the spinach in the remaining butter; add to the fish. Warm gently to allow all the flavours to mingle and serve on a warmed platter. Fish is always better moistened with a little sauce, so if it reduces too much, simply add a little wine and melted butter.

Serve with a dry, full-flavoured white wine such as Vernaccia from San Gimignano, or a white from Pitigliano.

Bartolomeo Sacchi described sole as "a delicately flavoured fish, not very long and as thin as the sole of a shoe, from which the name probably derives. It is also considered a high quality fish".

Preparation time:
20 minutes.
Cooking time:
20 minutes.
800 g fillets of sole
plain white flour
80 g butter
one glass white wine
1.2 kg spinach
salt.

Contorni

Vegetables

Cicoria

Rucola

Valeriana

Portulaca

Lattuga

Radicchio

▼

Insalata

Salad

Carefully wash all the salad leaves, dry thoroughly and chop finely. Put in a large salad bowl and add the dressing. For a perfectly mixed and dressed salad, first sprinkle with salt, then add just a small quantity of vinegar and toss well. Now add the oil and toss again thoroughly to combine all the flavours. If you prefer, you can also prepare the dressing separately. Whisk the oil, salt and vinegar together in a bowl, pour over the salad and toss. Depending on the season, you can make a mixed salad adding thin slices of fennel or fresh baby courgettes, green celery, cress and tomatoes. For a quick and handy summer lunch, add some chopped, diced pecorino or other tasty hard cheese, or flaked Parmesan to the salad.

Pliny the Elder recounted that, "The Emperor Augustus recovered from a serious illness by eating only salad". Apicius suggested, "Dress salad leaves, fresh from the field, with garum, oil and vinegar". Bartolomeo Sacchi claimed that "Rocket is an amazing stimulus to the pleasures of Venus".

Preparation time:
20 minutes.
A good mixture of various kinds
of salad such as radicchio,
endive, rocket, chicory,
valerian, lettuce
extra-virgin olive oil
salt
wine vinegar.

Cleaning and preparing vegetables

In *Il Trinciante* (The Carver) Vincenzo Cervio explains in great detail "How to chop artichokes". The lengthy description might seem a bit exaggerated at first, but in fact their correct preparation is essential to the successful outcome of a recipe.

Firstly, always choose fresh artichokes. Chop off all but a centimetre of the stem (the stems can also be used for cooking if you peel them, removing the outer, dark green flesh). Now remove the hard, darker outer leaves, until you get to the heart of the artichoke where the bottom of the leaves, near to the stem, are a very light green in colour. Trim off the spiny, upper tips of the leaves. Cut the artichoke in two and scrape out the fuzzy, inner 'choke' with a knife. Cut into segments or slice, according to the recipe you are following, and put in a bowl with water and a good squeeze of lemon juice to prevent discoloration. Drain well before cooking. Other vegetables do not need so much preparation: simply remove the tougher, outer leaves, stems or roots; peel or shell, and they can be washed, chopped and cooked according to your recipe. Here is a useful tip though: vegetables which grow underground (root vegetables) should be put in cold water to cook, while

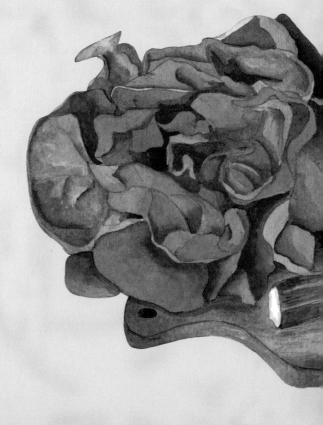

those which grow above ground should be dropped into boiling water. The heat and the cooking process tend to reduce the vitamin content, but you can reduce the loss by using only a little water or, even better, by steaming them. Salad should be washed in water with a teaspoon of bicarbonate of soda dissolved in it. This makes it easier to wash, and removes any bugs or insects attached to the leaves. Rinse at least four times in fresh, cold water before draining and drying the leaves.

▼

Fagioli o ceci all'olio

Beans or chick-peas in oil

*Preparation time:
5 minutes.
Cooking time:
2 hours.
700 g beans or
chick-peas (double
the quantity if fresh)
salt
bunch of sage
2 garlic cloves
extra-virgin olive oil.*

Chick-peas and beans are absolutely essential ingredients in Florentine cookery. Follow just a few, simple rules when cooking, and they will always be perfectly tender and delicious. Rinse them carefully in a sieve or colander and cover with plenty of cold water (you will need about three litres). Add a pinch of salt, sage leaves and the garlic and leave to cook over a very low flame. They usually need about two hours, though if fresh, only forty minutes, but stir them with a wooden spoon to test how soft they are. Serve with plenty of good olive oil, if possible, newly-pressed.

Do not serve beans if there are already vegetables (apart from salad) in any of the other courses. Many cooks believe it is better to soak beans or peas in cold water with two teaspoons of bicarbonate of soda for at least eight hours

first. I think that slow cooking over a very low flame gives better results, but you can try different methods to discover which works best for you.

Fagioli all'uccelletto

Beans in tomato sauce

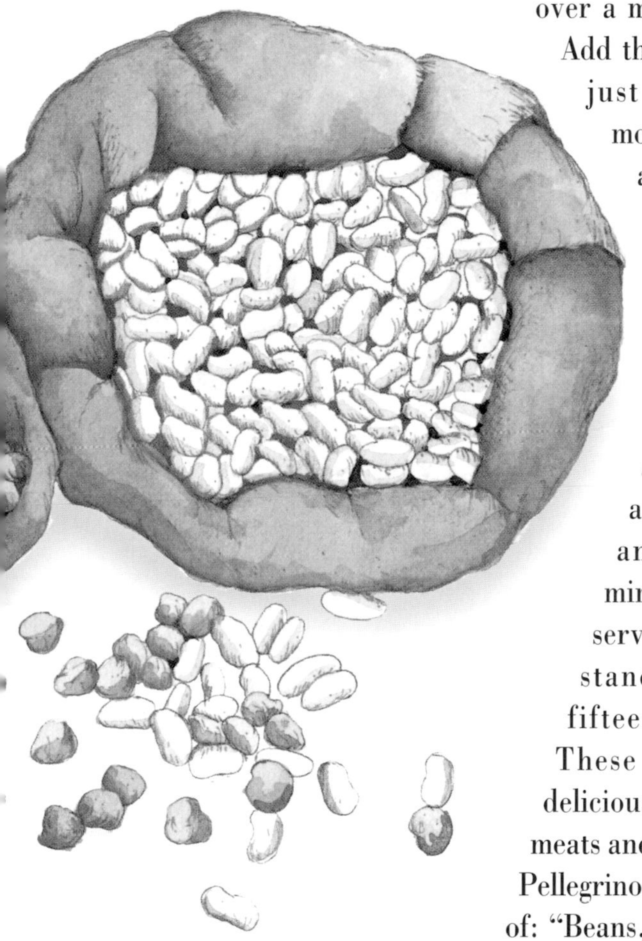

over a medium heat. Add the beans with just a little moisture, cover and cook for five minutes to let the flavours come out. Add the puréed tomatoes, salt and pepper and cook for another ten minutes. Before serving, leave to stand for about fifteen minutes. These beans are delicious with boiled meats and sausages. Pellegrino Artusi wrote of: "Beans, cooked with the same ingredients as for small birds. These beans are a good accompaniment for boiled meat, if you don't want to eat them on their own".

Preparation time:
10 minutes.
Cooking time:
two hours 30 minutes.
Standing time:
15 minutes.
600 g dried
cannellini beans
4 tbsp extra-virgin
olive oil
300 g tomatoes
garlic
sage
salt
black pepper.

Cook the beans as described in the previous recipe. Put the oil, garlic and sage into a large saucepan and warm

▼

Piselli novelli in casseruola

Casseroled new peas

*Preparation time:
15 minutes.
Cooking time:
20 minutes.
3 kg fresh peas
50 g streaky bacon,
in one piece
3 tbsp extra-virgin
olive oil
parsley
2 cloves of garlic
pinch of salt.*

Shell the fresh new peas; their weight will reduce to about one kilo. Chop the bacon into small cubes and fry in the oil in an earthenware casserole. Wash and drain the peas, pour into the casserole and then add fresh parsley tied into a bunch, garlic (fresh garlic is at its best in May), a pinch of salt and two glasses of water. Cook, covered, for twenty minutes. Remove the garlic and parsley and serve tepid.

This is a speciality in springtime when tiny, tender, sweet new peas are available. They are ideal not only with stuffed rabbit but also with roast pork, peppery stew and braised beef.

Rape

Turnip greens

For perfect results the vegetable greens must be properly prepared and cleaned. Remove the large, tough yellow leaves and the stalks. You should have about 1.5 kg of leaves after discarding and cleaning.

Wash carefully and chop them; warm the oil and garlic in a large saucepan and add the chopped leaves.

Add a glass of water, salt and a pinch of chili pepper. Cover and leave to cook over a medium heat for twenty minutes until the water evaporates completely. Taste and adjust for salt before serving. You might sometimes be able to buy the turnip leaves on their own. If so, clean, trim and wash them, put into boiling, salted water and cook for about thirty minutes; after draining thoroughly, sauté in oil with garlic and chili pepper.

The *Anonimo Toscano* wrote "On turnips. Cut the heads of the turnips off, then chop them and boil in water".

Preparation time:
20 minutes.
Cooking time:
20 minutes.
2 kg turnip heads or leaves
4 tbsp extra-virgin
olive oil
3 cloves of garlic
salt
chili pepper.

▼

Fritto misto

Mixed fried vegetables

Preparation time:
30 minutes.
Cooking time:
20 minutes.
Artichokes, courgettes,
aubergines, onions,
asparagus, cauliflower,
courgette flowers, mushrooms
extra-virgin olive oil
salt.
For the batter
Preparation time:
5 minutes.
150 g plain flour
one tbsp extra-virgin
olive oil
salt.

Carefully clean and wash all the vegetables; dry and cut into pieces of roughly equal size (cut the onions and aubergines into rings, the courgettes vertically into sticks, the artichokes into segments, split the cauliflower into single florets. You only need to remove the stalks of the asparagus and the courgette flowers. Clean the mushroom caps with a damp cloth, trim away the root end and scrape the stalk lightly with a knife. The mushrooms should only be coated with flour before frying. Prepare the batter as follows: using a wooden spoon beat together the flour, oil, salt and just enough water to make a fairly thick paste which should be smooth and creamy, leaving ribbon-like trails when it falls from the spoon. If

you like a frothier batter, replace the water with the same amount of beer, or use half water and half beer. Put the batter in the fridge for an hour before using it to coat the vegetables. The greater

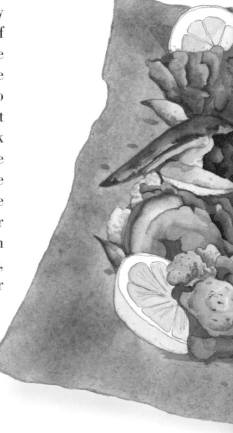

the difference between the temperature of the hot oil and that of the cold batter, the crisper the fry will be.

Dip the vegetables into the batter and fry in plenty of oil over a medium heat, until light golden. Do not allow them to become too dark in colour as this will give the fry a slightly bitter taste. Drain and place the fried vegetables on kitchen paper to dry and serve hot, sprinkled with salt.

Pellegrino Artusi commented, "This is the method they use in Tuscany and it is the best. There they use and abuse vegetables and greens to such an extent, that they have learned to cook them better than anywhere else".

▼

Patate lesse

Boiled potatoes

Preparation time:
5 minutes.
Cooking time:
30 minutes.
One kg white potatoes
water
extra-virgin olive oil
parsley
salt.

Put the potatoes in a large saucepan with plenty of cold water. Bring to the boil, add the salt and cook for about thirty minutes; turn off the heat. Drain, leave until tepid then peel and cut into fairly thick slices. Arrange on a serving dish, sprinkle with parsley and drizzle some oil over. If you like garlic, chop a whole clove and add to the potatoes. In the summertime you can also eat these potatoes cold, as a salad. Boiled potatoes are also very tasty reheated: I prefer them tossed in butter, with a little diced bacon and a handful of grated Parmesan, until golden brown on both sides. Turn them over as if they were an omlette to brown on the other side.

Purè di patate

Mashed potatoes

Boil the potatoes until cooked, peel and pass through a potato ricer, or mash well. Warm the milk in a pan and add the potatoes to it. Cook slowly for ten minutes, stirring continuously; taste for salt and add more milk if necessary (a purée should be neither too runny nor too thick). Finally, add the butter, stir through and serve hot.

Purée can be reheated too: beat an egg and mix through the potatoes with some grated Parmesan and some chopped up bacon. Put into a buttered oven-proof dish and dust with breadcrumbs. Cook in the oven at 180° C for fifteen minutes.

*Preparation time:
15 minutes.
Cooking time:
45 minutes.
One kg potatoes
one litre milk
salt
40 g butter.*

Patate fritte

Fried potatoes

Preparation time:
10 minutes.
Cooking time:
20 minutes.
One kg potatoes
extra-virgin olive oil
salt.
Optional:
garlic
rosemary
sage.

Peel a kilo of potatoes, wash them and cut into evenly-sized pieces. Warm a generous amount of oil in a frying pan, add the potatoes and cook over a high flame for three minutes. Put the lid on the pan and cook for a further ten minutes over a low heat. Remove the lid, turn the potatoes very carefully so that they do not break, increase the heat and fry for another five minutes. The potatoes are ready when they are crispy and golden on the outside. Lift out of the oil and drain on kitchen paper.

Transfer to a warm serving dish and sprinkle with salt just before eating. During the last five minutes of cooking you can add garlic, rosemary or sage to the potatoes to give them a delicious flavour, but remember to remove the herbs before serving.

You can also reuse fried potatoes by putting them in the sauces of meat casseroles such as braised beef, stew, peppery stew, beef rolls, meat loaf and rissoles.

▼

Patate e cipolle

Potatoes and onions

Peel both the onions and potatoes, wash and cut into thickish slices. Put into an ovenproof dish in alternate layers and season with the oil, rosemary and salt. Cook in the oven at 180° C for thirty minutes. Check they are crispy and golden, remove from the oven and serve warm. This dish is really rather filling in itself. Never serve it after an onion soup, for example, or with a substantial main course such as peppery stew or T-bone steak. In the winter-time you could even serve it as a first course.

Preparation time: 20 minutes. Cooking time: 30 minutes. One kg potatoes one kg onions extra-virgin olive oil fresh rosemary salt.

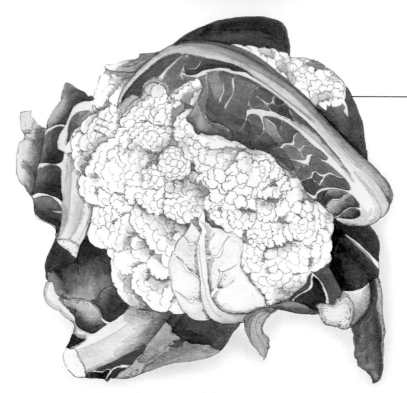

Cavolfiore stufato

Stewed cauliflower

Preparation time:
15 minutes.
Cooking time:
20 minutes.
One kg cauliflower
garlic cloves
3 tbsp extra-virgin
olive oil
200 g tomatoes
salt.

Parboil the cauliflower for five minutes in salted water (or cook in a steamer for ten minutes) then break it into florets. Put the garlic and oil into a large pan or flameproof dish, heat through and then add the cauliflower, turning it over gently. When it is well softened (about ten minutes) add the puréed tomatoes and then cover. Cook together gently for five minutes so that the flavours combine, taste for salt,

remove the garlic and serve hot. Cauliflower is usually parboiled in order to reduce the smell which many find too strong. If, however, the odour doesn't bother you, simply fry the florets in the oil and garlic without parboiling. Cover the pan and cook over a medium heat, gradually adding a few drops of warm water, if necessary. The *Anonimo Toscano* gave instructions for "How to make well-cooked white

▼

Asparagi

Asparagus

Trim away almost all the white end of the asparagus stalks. Wash the spears well, tie together into a bunch and put into a tall saucepan, standing upright, to steam. Remove from the heat when they are still fairly firm, arrange in an oven-proof dish, pour over the melted butter and sprinkle with salt and grated Parmesan. Put in the oven until crisp and golden.

If you do not want to bake the asparagus, then steam them until completely cooked and serve with a simple and delicious sauce made of oil, lemon juice and salt whisked together for five minutes. Asparagus are good for the digestion and they are also diuretic. Apicius advised, "Let the asparagus dry thoroughly and then put them into hot water again: this makes them firmer". As for the *Anonimo Toscano*, he wrote "On the sparaci".

Preparation time:
10 minutes.
Cooking time:
30 minutes.
2 kg asparagus
100 g butter
100 g Parmesan
salt.

▼

Carciofi ritti

Roman-style artichokes

*Preparation time:
30 minutes.
Cooking time:
30 minutes.
9 fresh artichokes
3 tbsp extra-virgin
olive oil
salt
thyme.*

Clean the artichokes and put them in water with lemon juice until ready to use. Spread the leaves open and, holding upside down, press the head firmly down on the work surface to force them further open. Warm the oil in an aluminium saucepan and put the artichokes in with the stems pointing upwards. Add salt, increase the heat, cover and cook until well browned (about seven minutes). Add a glass of water and leave until completely cooked, checking that the sauce does not dry out completely, as it should be poured over the artichokes before serving. Before removing from the heat, taste for salt and sprinkle fresh thyme leaves over or, if you prefer, parsley, either finely chopped or tied into a bunch. Present on a warmed serving dish.

Dolci

Cakes and desserts

CONVERSION TABLES

THESE ARE APPROXIMATE CONVERSIONS WHICH MAY HAVE BEEN ROUNDED UP OR DOWN SLIGHTLY.

Metric	Imperial	USA Cups	
Grams	UK lbs/oz	USACups	UK/Spoons
10 g	1/4 oz		1 1/2 tsp
50 g	2 oz	1/4	4 tbsp
100 g	3 1/2 oz	1/2	8 tbsp
150 g	5 oz	3/4	12 tbsp
200 g	7 oz	1	16 tbsp
250 g	9 oz	1 1/3	
300 g	11 oz	1 1/2	
350 g	12 oz	1 3/4	
400 g	14 oz	2	
500 g	1 lb	2	
1 kg	2 lb	4	
1 1/2 kg	3 lb	6 1/2	
2 kg	4 lb	9	

°Celsius	°Fahrenheit	Gas Mark
160	300	2
180	350	4
200	400	6

Litres	Pints	Cups
1/2	1	2
1	2	4
1 1/2	3	6

Centimetres	Inches
1	0,4
10	4,0

Schiacciata alla fiorentina

Florentine sponge cake

Put the sifted flour, baking powder, oil, milk, grated orange rind, saffron, sugar, eggs, and a pinch of salt into a mixing bowl and beat together thoroughly until all the lumps are eliminated and the batter is smooth and thick. Grease a shallow rectangular baking pan and pour in the mixture (the schiacciata should be about 2 cm high). Put into a pre-heated oven at 150° C for half an hour. Sprinkle plenty of icing sugar on top when cool. You can also put a stencil on top of the cake before sprinkling with icing sugar to make designs.

If you are very sweet-toothed, you can cut the cake in two and fill it with whipped cream, chocolate icing, chocolate cream or any other sweet filling or spread you like.

This light sponge is traditionally made during Carneval time, in February. Originally lard was used, but I have replaced it with oil as this makes a lighter cake. But if you are not worried about your cholesterol level, then why not try the flavour of the original recipe?

Preparation time:
15 minutes.
Cooking time:
30 minutes.
250 g plain white flour
4 tbsp extra-virgin
olive oil
(or 50 g lard)
one glass milk
one orange
half a teaspoon
powdered saffron
90 g sugar
2 eggs
2 teaspoons
baking powder
icing sugar
salt.

Schiacciata con l'uva

Sweet grape bread

Preparation time:
30 minutes.
Raising time for dough:
2 hours.
Cooking time:
40 minutes.
For the dough:
25 g dried yeast
350 g plain white flour
4 tbsp extra-virgin
olive oil
100 g sugar
salt.
To garnish:
one kg black grapes
sugar
extra-virgin olive oil
rosemary.

Dissolve the yeast in a little tepid water and add to the flour, oil, two tablespoons sugar and a pinch of salt in a large bowl.
Mix together rapidly, form into a round ball, cover the bowl with a cloth and leave to rise in a warm place for two hours. Using small, black wine grapes and not the larger, table variety, carefully remove the grapes from their individual stalks, put in a colander, wash and leave to dry.
Divide the dough in two and roll out into rectangles the same size as the baking tray you are using. Put one piece in the greased tray and top with half of the grapes. Sprinkle with a little sugar and put the second rectangle of dough on top. Cover with the remaining grapes and a little sugar.
Warm some oil with rosemary leaves in it and drizzle over the top of the schiacciata. Put in the oven at 180° C. and cook for about forty minutes.

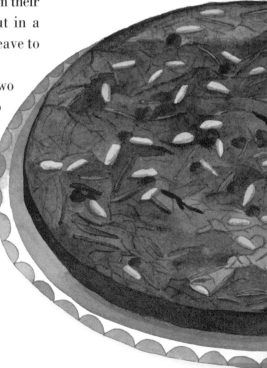

Castagnaccio

Chestnut cake

Sift the chestnut flour into a mixing bowl and gradually add 800 ml of water, whisking continually to avoid lumps forming, until you have a smooth paste, neither too runny nor too thick, but forming ribbons when it falls from the spoon. Soak the raisins and squeeze out the excess water. Add two tablespoons of oil, a pinch of salt, the raisins, pinenuts and shelled walnuts to the batter. Pour the mixture into a shallow, greased baking tray (the cake should only be about 1 cm high), sprinkle some rosemary leaves on top and drizzle a tablespoon of oil over. Put in the oven for thirty minutes. Leave aside for about half an hour before serving as the cake should be eaten either tepid or cold. For many centuries chestnuts were part of the staple diet in mountainous and hilly areas and for the poorer classes in general as they provided an inexpensive form of nutrition. The original, Florentine version of *castagnaccio*, which is also known as *migliaccio* (black pudding) in some parts of Tuscany, had only pinenuts in it. This recipe is a combination of traditional recipes from both Pistoia and Lucca which I find slightly tastier.

Preparation time:
20 minutes.
Cooking time:
30 minutes.
Standing time:
30 minutes.
600 g chestnut flour
3 tbsp extra-virgin
olive oil
salt
70 g raisins
40 g pinenuts
40 g walnuts
rosemary.

Bongo

Chocolate profiteroles

Preparation time: 30 minutes.
Cooking time: 40 minutes.
For about 35 profiteroles:
60 g butter
300 ml water
salt
125 g plain white flour
4 eggs
800 g whipping cream
icing sugar
150 g dark chocolate.

Put the water in a large saucepan, add the butter, and let it melt. Add a pinch of salt, sift the flour well and throw it in all at once. Stir immediately and thoroughly until it forms an elastic mixture and then continue to cook and stir for about fifteen minutes.

When all the water has been absorbed and the paste is quite smooth and even, coming away easily from the sides and bottom of the saucepan, remove from the heat. Leave to cool well and then add the eggs one at a time, beating in well. Put the mixture into a pastry bag with a large nozzle and squeeze profiteroles out onto a greased baking tray. Put in the oven at 180° C for twenty minutes. In the meantime whip half the cream and sweeten with icing sugar. Put it into a piping bag and fill the profiteroles when they have cooled sufficiently. Melt the chocolate over a bain-marie, let it cool and then add to the remaining lightly whipped cream. Drop the profiteroles into the chocolate cream one by one and arrange in a pyramid on a serving dish. Decorate with rosettes of whipped cream. Originally profiteroles were fried rather than baked; the Florentine recipe was introduced to France where it was known as pâtes à chaud, "hot buns".

Cenci

Sweet fritters

Mix the flour, eggs, sugar, Vin Santo, grated lemon rind, three tablespoons of oil and a pinch of salt in a large bowl. Knead well, forming the pastry into a ball and roll out on a pastry board to a thickness of about two millimetres. Cut into ribbons about eight centimetres wide and then cut obliquely into sections. Fill a frying pan with oil, heat and drop the pastry in. When the cenci become crisp and golden, remove, put them on kitchen paper to dry well and then shake plenty of icing sugar over. You can make the biscuits look prettier by cutting the ribbons with a pastry wheel, or you can use your own imagination to cut it into different shapes and forms.

Roll the pastry out as often as necessary to use it all up. Cenci, like the Florentine schiacciata, are traditional Carneval time biscuits. They are found throughout all of northern and central Italy, and have different names according to the region. In Bologna, for example, they are called *frappole* (fringes) and in Milan, *chiacchiere* (chatters).

Preparation time:
30 minutes.
Cooking time:
15 minutes.
400 g plain white flour
2 eggs
3 dessert spoons sugar
half a glass Vin Santo
(or sweet sherry)
one lemon
extra-virgin olive oil
icing sugar
salt.

▼

Bomboloni

Doughnuts

Preparation time:
30 minutes.
Standing time for the dough:
3 hours
Cooking time:
15 minutes.
25 g dried yeast
200 g milk
100 g sugar
salt
500 g plain white flour
one lemon
2 teaspoons vanilla flavouring
80 g butter
extra-virgin olive oil
salt.

Put the dried yeast, warmed milk, half of the sugar and a pinch of salt into a bowl and mix together carefully with a wooden spoon. Transfer to a baking bowl and add the sifted flour, grated rind of half the lemon, vanilla and the melted butter.

Work the dough well until smooth and elastic. Cover and leave to rise in a warm place for two hours.

Roll the dough out to a thickness of about one centimetre; use a glass to cut out rounds about five centimetres in diameter. Gather up the remaining pieces, roll out and cut more rounds until you have used up all the dough. Cover with a cloth and leave to rise a further hour. Fry in plenty of hot oil, turning until golden on both sides. Remove the doughnuts one by one, drain on kitchen paper and sprinkle with the sugar.

If you like, you can fill them with jam, confectioner's custard or chocolate cream.

▼

Tiramisù

Coffee and mascarpone cream

Beat the egg yolks and sugar together until thick and frothy; add the mascarpone and blend carefully. Whisk the egg whites until firm and fold through, mixing well. Dip the savoy biscuits into the coffee and whisky and line a rectangular serving dish with a single layer.

Spread a good helping of the mascarpone cream on top and sprinkle with cocoa powder. Repeat the layers until all the cream is used up. Put in the fridge for at least an hour before serving. You can adapt this recipe to make a speedy and delicious dessert in individual goblets. Make the mascarpone cream, crumble three amaretti biscuits into each goblet and top with a helping of the cream.

This is not originally a Florentine recipe, but it has become one of the most popular desserts throughout Italy, especially in winter time. It is best made the day before and left in the fridge overnight to let the flavours mingle well.

Preparation time:
20 minutes.
Refrigeration time:
24 hours.
4 eggs
150 g sugar
500 g mascarpone
300 g savoy biscuits or lady-fingers
3 tablespoons espresso coffee
2 tablespoons whisky
cocoa powder.

▼

Zuccotto

Zuccotto

Preparation time: 40 minutes.
Cooking time: 10 minutes.
Refrigeration time: 6 hours.
400 g sponge cake
500 ml whipping cream
icing sugar
maraschino liqueur
100 g dark chocolate
50 g chocolate drops
50 g candied lime and orange peel.

Cut three-quarters of the sponge cake into rectangles and use to line a pudding bowl. Brush the pieces of sponge with the liqueur. Whip the cream and sweeten with the icing sugar.

Melt the chocolate over a bain-marie; when it has cooled, add half the whipped cream, mix together and then pour into the pudding bowl; smooth the surface.

Stir the chocolate drops and mixed candied peel into the remaining whipped cream and pour into the pudding bowl. Now cover the open top of the bowl with the remaining pieces of sponge cake and seal with a sheet of greaseproof paper. Leave in the fridge for six hours.

To remove the zuccotto from the bowl before serving, dip it into hot water for a few minutes, then cover with a flat serving dish and turn upside down.

The best wines to accompany this sweet are an Aleatico from Elba or a good Vin Santo.

Torta di mele

Apple flan

In a large bowl mix together the yoghurt, flour, sugar, eggs, oil, grated lemon rind, yeast and four of the apples, peeled and chopped finely. Grease and flour a cake tin and put the remaining sliced apples in the bottom. Sprinkle with lemon juice and sugar.

Pour the mixture on top and put in the oven to cook at 180° C for thirty minutes. Sprinkle the surface with icing sugar before serving if liked. This flan is delicious just slightly warm but it can also be eaten hot with vanilla ice cream, or cold with hot custard.

Bramleys are the best apples for this recipe, otherwise use a juicy and slightly sharp apple which bakes well. Domenico Romoli's recipe was for, "Pie with pears and apples beneath".

Preparation time:
30 minutes.
Cooking time:
40 minutes.
One natural yoghurt
150 g plain white flour
120 g sugar
3 eggs
3 tbsp extra-virgin
olive oil
one lemon
two teaspoons
powdered yeast
6 apples.

▼

Quaresimali

Lenten biscuits

Preparation time:
20 minutes.
Cooking time:
10 minutes.
3 eggs
150 g icing sugar
100 g plain flour
50 g cocoa powder
salt.

Whisk the egg whites until stiff and stir in the sugar, sifted flour and cocoa powder with a pinch of salt. Fill a pastry bag with the mixture and 'write' the letters of the alphabet onto a buttered baking tray. Leave plenty of space between the biscuits as they will spread during cooking and might join together. Bake in the oven for ten minutes at 150° C. They are ready when they turn an attractive golden brown colour.

These biscuits are typical, fatless Lenten fare, as their name suggests.

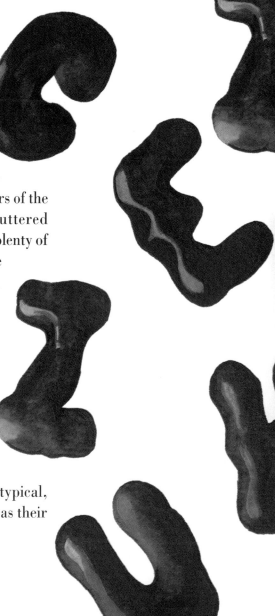

Pinocchiati

Pine nut crisps

Remove from the heat and add the shelled pine nuts stirring briskly all the time. Place the circles of rice paper on your working surface and spread even quantities of the mixture on top of each piece. Leave until completely cool before serving. Instead of individual biscuits, you could make one large round using a single, circular piece of rice paper. Spread all the mixture on top and cut into small pieces. This recipe is uniquely Florentine in origin. Sweet morsels, such as pinocchiati, were a typical starter to meals during the Renaissance. Today they can still be found in Umbria where they also add cocoa powder to the recipe. They are perfect little tea-time nibbles on dull, rainy afternoons.

Heat the sugar with half a glass of water in a saucepan.

Dissolve the sugar completely over a low heat and cook until the mixture thickens. Take care not to let the sugar burn.

Preparation time: 30 minutes.
Cooking time: 15 minutes.
500 g sugar
300 g pine nuts
20 circles of rice paper about 5 cm in diameter.

▼

Crespelle dolci

Sweet pancakes

Preparation time:
20 minutes.
Cooking time:
15 minutes.
2 eggs
125 g plain flour
salt
250 ml milk
30 g butter
sugar
cinnamon powder
a few fresh mint leaves
icing sugar.

Beat the eggs in a bowl, add the sifted flour and a pinch of salt and mix well. Slowly add the milk, the melted butter and a tablespoon of sugar. Pour about four tablespoonfuls at a time into a greased, heavy-bottomed frying pan and fry on both sides. Fold the pancakes into four and put on a serving plate; dust with icing sugar and cinnamon powder and decorate with the leaves of mint. You can also serve the pancakes with this delicious fruit sauce: - over a medium heat gradually thicken half a kilo of mixed berries (b l u e b e r r i e s, b l a c k b e r r i e s, blackcurrants, bilberries etc.) with a tablespoon of sugar and a tablespoon of maraschino liqueur. Dissolve a little cornflour or starch in a few drops of water and

add to the sauce. Leave to cool.
This recipe can be found in the manuscript of Cristoforo Messi Sbugo: "To make forty Florentine egg fritters, filled or empty".

▼

Frittelle

Fritters

Cook the rice in the milk, stirring frequently to prevent it sticking. Stir in the peel of one lemon and leave to stand for twelve hours. Soak the raisins and squeeze the excess liquid out. Remove the lemon peel from the rice and add the butter, flour, raisins, Vin Santo, sugar and grated orange and lemon peel. Stir in the egg yolks, whisk the egg whites until they form firm peaks and add to the cold rice mixture.

Warm plenty oil in a frying pan, add spoonfuls of the mixture and fry until golden and crispy.

Drain on kitchen paper and sprinkle with sugar.

In Florence these tasty little 'sweets' are traditionally eaten on the 19th of March, Saint Joseph's feast day, and therefore also Father's Day. They are excellent with a good, sweet Vin Santo.

Preparation time:
20 minutes.
Standing time:
12 hours.
Cooking time:
20 minutes.
One litre milk
300 g rice such as
Italian Arborio
50 g butter
2 tbsp plain flour
100 g raisins
one glass Vin Santo
150 g sugar
one orange and two lemons
2 eggs
extra-virgin olive oil.

Sorbetto

Sorbet

Preparation time:
20 minutes.
Cooking time:
2 minutes.
Standing time:
10 minutes.
Refrigeration time:
6 hours.
200 g sugar
4 lemons or oranges
half a litre water
one egg
sage or mint leaves.

Put the water and sugar in a saucepan and boil over a medium heat for about two minutes, until it turns into a syrup. Skim, then add the juice and grated rind of the oranges or lemons. Leave aside for ten minutes, strain and put into a dish; leave until quite cold. Whisk the egg whites until stiff and add to the syrup.

Put in the freezer for about six hours, remembering to take it out to stir well every half hour. Decorate each portion with sage or mint leaves before serving.

This unusual sweet dates back to at least the 13th century and was always served at the banquets of the Medici. Ice-houses were built in the area of Santa Maria Novella for its production. It was generally served as a sweet, however, if the meal consisted of many different dishes, it was served as a welcome and refreshing pause between the first and second courses. Lemon and orange trees were widely grown and used ornamentally in many of the city's gardens.

Merende

Snacks

Perfect daily bread

These days it might seem something of an anachronism to dedicate an entire section to the ancient art of bread making. However, I thought it was a shame to ignore such an important part of our diet, not only common to every nation but also, after all, the basis of many more imaginative recipes.

1. Make sure that all the ingredients are at the right temperature; they should be kept cool at around 18° C.
2. Prepare a basic yeast dough mixture as follows: pour a mound of flour onto the work surface and make a well in the centre; dissolve the yeast in some tepid water and pour into the well. Work the liquid into the flour and knead until you obtain a soft, elastic dough; leave aside.
3. Cover with a cloth and put in a dry, draught-free place to rise.
4. The dough has risen completely when it has doubled in bulk.
5. If adding spices or herbs, these should be finely chopped or powdered.
6. It is a good idea to put a shallow bowl of water beneath the bread while it is baking. This produces steam which not only helps the bread to rise but also prevents a hard crust forming immediately and perhaps even burning.
7. Bread should be eaten when it has cooled completely.
8. The bigger the loaf of bread, the better and longer it will keep.

Preparation time: 30 minutes. Raising time for the dough: 2 hours. Baking time: about 30 minutes.

500 g plain white flour, 30 g dried yeast, 250 ml water, 3 tablespoons extra-virgin olive oil, 10 g salt.

Sadly, hardly anyone makes their own homemade bread anymore, and yet it really is good idea to try at least once in your life just for the fun of it. The feeling of pleasure and satisfaction you experience when you take your very own crispy loaf out of the oven is unique and yet as old as time, indeed it is not too much to say that it is really quite moving.

To make the dough, dissolve the yeast in a large bowl with some warm water. Add the oil, salt and flour and mix together thoroughly. Turn out on to a work surface and knead well; form into a ball and leave to rise, covered, in a warm place for two hours. The bulk of the dough will increase visibly once the yeast begins to work. Once risen, put the dough on a floured work surface and divide into the shapes and sizes you desire. Bake the bread in an oven pre-heated to 200° C. The time required for baking depends on the size of the loaves you are making, but in general the bread is ready when it is an even golden-brown colour and hollow-sounding when tapped on top. Turn the oven off and leave the bread to cool with the door half open to avoid any moisture forming.

Bread snacks

Bread, oil and vinegar
Pour some extra-virgin olive oil on each slice of bread, sprinkle with salt and add two drops of wine vinegar.

Bread, oil and tomato
Cut a fresh tomato in two and squeeze the halves over slices of bread until they become red; add a pinch of salt and pour some extra-virgin olive oil on top.

Bread, butter and anchovies
Spread butter on each slice and top with chopped anchovy fillets.

Bread, butter and jam
Spread with butter, and top with fruit jam.

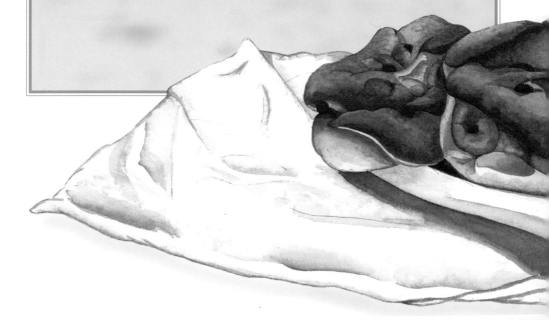

▼

Pandiramerino

Rosemary bread

Dissolve the yeast with a little warm water in a mixing bowl. Add the sifted flour, three tablespoons of oil, the sugar and some more warm water. Mix together briskly, form into a ball and leave to rise for two hours. Heat two tablespoons of oil and the washed and dried fresh rosemary leaves in a small saucepan. Remove from the heat and add the sultanas. When the oil has cooled, mix and knead well into the raised dough. Make into six buns, arrange on a baking tray dusted with flour and leave to rise for another half hour. Mark the top of each bun with a cross, brush with oil and bake in the oven at 180°C. for thirty minutes. *Ramerino* is the vernacular word for rosemary and originally these rosemary-flavoured buns were a speciality prepared on Easter Thursday. Now they are made all year round, however, and Florentines eat these fragrant buns as a tasty mid-morning snack.

Preparation time:
30 minutes.
Raising time:
two hours 30 minutes.
Baking time:
30 minutes.
25 g dried yeast
400 g plain white flour
extra-virgin olive oil
50 g sugar
rosemary
150 g sultanas.

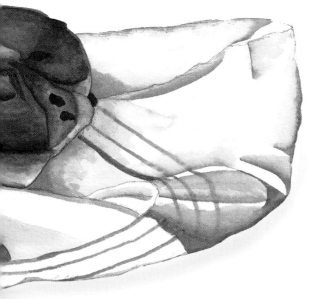

▼

Schiacciata con l'olio

Flat bread with oil

Prepare the dough following the recipe for basic bread dough. Roll out fairly flat (about 2 cm) to make either one large or two smaller oblong-shaped *schiacciate*. Put in a baking tray lightly dusted with flour and make dimples about six centimetres apart by pressing your finger well down into the dough. Sprinkle with plenty of salt and drizzle the surface with olive oil. Bake in an oven pre-heated to 200° C. for 15 minutes.

Schiacciata is often flavoured with slices of tomato or courgettes, with rosemary or any other fresh herb. Simply top the dough with the herbs or chopped vegetables before putting it into the oven.

Ricotta e cioccolato

Ricotta and chocolate

Preparation time: 10 minutes.
300 g ricotta made from cow's or sheep's milk chocolate cream finger biscuits.

Put the ricotta into dessert goblets and top with spoonfuls of chocolate cream or spread. Decorate with the finger biscuits and serve. Instead of the chocolate cream you can use just normal sugar sprinkled on top, honey or jam (blackcurrent is perhaps best as it is quite delicate and will not overwhelm the flavour of the ricotta).

If at all possible, use genuine, fresh whole-milk ricotta. It is not always easy to find, but the natural flavour, aroma and softness of the cheese is reminiscent of the farm produce of bygone days.

Zabaione

Zabaglione

Beat the egg whites in a bowl until they form stiff peaks. In another, larger bowl beat the yolks and sugar together until frothy, creamy and pale yellow. Add the egg whites to the yolks and blend thoroughly until the mixture is smooth and even; add the Vin Santo. Serve in dessert goblets with the biscuits.

This dish is rather rich and filling and is therefore a good snack for children who have lost their appetite or for those whose work is physically demanding. Luckily, children also love it, though I would suggest leaving out the Vin Santo or sherry...

Pellegrino Artusi wrote, "I wish all children's food were as harmless as this, for there would certainly be fewer nervy and hysterical people around today if it were".

6 eggs
200 g sugar
100 ml dry Vin Santo
(or sherry)
finger biscuits.

Sottolio

Preserves

▼

Pomodori

Tomatoes

In August choose good, well-ripened Florentine tomatoes, cut them in half, salt them well, place on a wooden board or surface and leave them in the sun until they have dried completely.

Arrange them, one on top of the other, in glass preserving bottles, adding chopped parsley and garlic to each layer. Press them down well and cover completely with oil.

These tomatoes are delicious served with boiled meats. However, store them for at least two months before using and do not keep them for more than a year after bottling. As with all preserves, they should be kept in a cool, dry place after opening.

One kg Florentine tomatoes (large and flattish, rather than round, with deep folds at the stalk)
salt
parsley
garlic
extra-virgin olive oil.

Zucchine

Courgettes

One kg courgettes
one litre white
wine vinegar
one litre water
garlic
rosemary
salt
extra-virgin olive oil.

Cut the courgettes into sticks about five centimetres long. Bring the water and vinegar to the boil and plunge in the chopped courgettes. Cook for fifteen minutes, drain and leave in the colander for twelve hours.

Put into a glass preserving bottle, interspersed with cloves of garlic, fresh rosemary leaves and a little salt. Cover with olive oil and close the bottle firmly.

Funghi

Mushrooms

One kg porcini mushrooms
half a litre wine vinegar
and half a litre white wine
salt
pepper
bay leaves
extra-virgin olive oil.

Choose firm, fresh, medium-sized mushrooms and separate the stalks from the caps. Using a sharp knife, scrape the stalks clean and then wipe with a cloth soaked in warm water. Wipe the caps with the damp cloth but do not scrape them. Cut the stalks in two both lengthwise and across; cut the caps into quarters. Bring a litre of water, the vinegar and the wine to the boil, add salt and drop in the mushrooms; cook for fifteen minutes. Drain well, leave to dry for twelve hours and put into glass preserving bottles with a little salt, some peppercorns and, if liked, a couple of bay leaves. Cover with oil and seal.

Carciofi

Artichokes

Only small artichokes of the best quality should be used for preserving; the darker, little *morellini* are best. Clean them thoroughly: remove the tough, outer leaves, peel away the green skin of the stalk and chop off the pointed tips. Put into water with some lemon juice to prevent browning. Bring the wine and vinegar to the boil with half a litre of water, add salt and cook the artichokes for twenty minutes. Drain and leave to dry well for twelve hours. Put into a glass preserving bottle, add salt and some black peppercorns and juniper berries. Cover with oil, but remember that the artichokes will absorb quite a lot, so it is best to wait a few hours before closing the bottles, then check the level of the oil and add some more if necessary.

one kg artichokes
lemon
one litre wine and
one litre white wine vinegar
salt
black pepper
juniper berries
extra-virgin olive oil.

Cavolfiore

Cauliflower

Choose a fairly large cauliflower, remove the outer leaves and break it into florets. Bring the water, vinegar and white wine to the boil and drop in the cauliflower. Cook for twenty minutes. Drain the cauliflower, leave to dry for twelve hours and arrange in a glass preserving bottle with the black peppercorns. Cover with oil and close tightly.

One kg cauliflower
half a litre wine vinegar and
half a litre white wine
salt
black pepper
extra-virgin olive oil.

How to taste wine

Wine is one of the most important elements in traditional Florentine culture and gastronomy; it would therefore be quite unthinkable not to dedicate some proper attention to this most harmonious and enjoyable partner at our table. In such a limited space, I can indicate only a few general guidelines which, if not followed, could spoil even the most delicious of meals.

1. Wines should be drunk in the following order: first the light, delicately-flavoured whites, then the more aromatic whites, rosés and lastly the reds, starting with the lighter and proceeding to more full-bodied.

2. Heavier and sweeter wines should never be served with red meats and game but with desserts and even well-matured, strongly-flavoured cheeses.

3. Drink some natural mineral water after tasting a wine in order to better appreciate the next one.

4. An entire meal can be based around one particularly rare or special wine.

5. The most important wines, such as Brunello or some of the Chianti Classico Riserva, must be served chambré at room temperature (20-22° C) - and opened at least an hour before serving. Very old wines should be decanted slowly and gently into a carafe or decanter.

To help you recognise the main varieties of wine produced in Tuscany, I have written brief, but hopefully adequate, descriptions of each major wine. I have also indicated the foods they best compliment. Do remember however, that such advice is not meant to be definitive as it can only be based on the overall, general characteristics of each kind of wine. For example, a particularly full-bodied Vernaccia from San Gimignano (several vintages come to mind) might be quite delicious with some of the more spicy, Tuscan cured hams.

Vino

Wine

...If there is anyone who does not like
Vernaccia
made from grapes gathered in
Pietrafitta,
damned
unnatural wretch,
get out of my sight!
Francesco Redi
Bacchus in Tuscany

Tuscan wines

Galestro

Colour: straw, with light green hues. **Bouquet**: delicately fruity with a suggestion of green apples. **Flavour**: dry and lively.
Temperature: serve at 8° C.
Suitable with: snacks and light meals.

Vernaccia di San Gimignano

Colour: pale yellow. **Bouquet**: delicate, lightly flowery.
Flavour: dry, harmonious, full-bodied. **Temperature**: serve at 10° C.
Suitable with: seafood, shellfish, salmon, sole and other delicately-flavoured fish, white meat.

Vin Santo

Colour: clear and golden with an amber hue.
Bouquet: pronounced yet refined. **Flavour**: warm, soft and full-bodied with a hint of sweetness.
Temperature: serve at 10° C.
Suitable with: fruit and desserts.

Aleatico dell'Elba

Colour: full, ruby red. **Bouquet**: sharp and subtle.
Flavour: warm and rich. **Temperature**: serve at 10° C.
Suitable with: this sweet wine can be drunk alone or with cakes and biscuits.

Chianti

Colour: bright, ruby red. **Bouquet**: good and grapey with a perfume of violets. **Flavour**: dry, smooth and velvety. **Temperature**: serve at 18° C.
Suitable with: almost all foods and meats.

Chianti Riserva

Riserva indicates a wine which has been aged at least three years.
Colour: deep red. **Bouquet**: full bodied and subtle, with a hint of
violets. **Flavour**: dry and flinty. **Temperature**: serve at 20-22° C;
the bottle should be opened an hour before serving.
Suitable with: roast red meats, duck, game and hard, mature
cheeses. The qualification Classico is applied to wines produced
in the heart of the Chianti area.

Vino Nobile di Montepulciano

Colour: deep garnet. **Bouquet**: delicate, with a hint of
violets. **Flavour**: dry and flinty.
Temperature: serve at 20° C; the bottle should be
opened an hour before serving. **Suitable with**: roast
meats, game and matured cheeses.
Vino Nobile di Montepulciano must be aged two
years before it can become a Riserva.

Brunello di Montalcino

Colour: deep red with garnet hues.
Bouquet: intriguing and harmonious.
Flavour: soft, velvety and smooth with a strong
hint of toasted almonds.
Temperature: serve at 20-22° C; the bottle
should be opened an hour before serving.
Suitable with: roast red meats and game.
Brunello is aged four years before selling and
becomes a Riserva after being aged for five years.

▼

Glossary

Al dente: firm to the bite. Pasta especially should never be overcooked and 'gluey'.

Antipasti: a light entrée eaten before the first course as an appetizer. They are very adaptable and, with increased quantities, may be eaten as a main course, generally for lunch.

Aubergine (G.B.): eggplant.

Au gratin: a dish topped with breadcrumbs or grated cheese, cooked in the oven and/or finished off under the grill until golden brown and toasted.

Bain marie: melting or cooking very gently by placing the ingredients in a bowl over a saucepan of simmering hot water.

Baste: moisten meat by pouring its own gravy or fat over.

Blanch: peeling by dropping into boiling water for a few seconds to loosen the skin.

Bouquet garni: a bunch of assorted herbs tied together and put into a stew, casserole or roast.

Braise: cooking slowly in liquid with onions, herbs, etc.

Bread: there is a great variety of Italian bread with many local variations. Generally Tuscan bread is 'country' style - a large, round loaf and unsalted. *Casalingo* literally means 'homemade' and is the term used for a typical, Tuscan unsalted loaf. *Salato* is salted bread, spongier and lighter. *Nero* means brown (usually wholemeal) bread. Stale bread is a frequent ingredient in Tuscan recipes, soaked in milk or water and then squeezed dry.

Courgettes (G.B.): zucchini.

Crostini: a slice of unsalted bread, topped with a variety of ingredients, from liver paste to chopped tomatoes, or boiled and sautéed green vegetables.

Decant: pour off by gently inclining the bottle without disturbing the sediment.

Fillet: a very tender, boneless piece of meat, or also fish.

Finocchiona: cold, cured pork, typically Tuscan and rather spicy, flavoured with fennel seeds.

Fontina: cheese from the Val d'Aosta, semi-soft, with a mild and slightly nutty flavour.

Frittata: omlette, but denser than the whisked, French version; it is always served whole and round or cut into pieces. In Florence it is often made with spinach and used as a sandwich filling.

Funghi porcini: one of the most delicious mushrooms, used fresh in the autumn and dried (soak for a couple of hours in cold water before using) the rest of the year. Their texture is smooth and silky and their flavour quite strong and distinctive. A genuine speciality and treat.

Garnish: decorate a dish for presentation at the table.

Hang: leave fresh meat, especially game, to dry or become tender.

Julienne: fine, matchstick-sized pieces of chopped vegetables.

Line: cover the inside of a dish, bowl or mould with paper, pastry, gelatine etc.

Parboil: cook partially to soften in boiling water before proceeding to cook in another manner.

Pecorino: cheese made with sheep's milk, ranging from the soft, fresh (young) kind to the more mature, harder, crumbly kind.

Peperoncino: chili pepper. In general the dried pods of the chili are used, crushed, in cooking.

Pinzimonio: a dish consisting of assorted, fresh, uncooked vegetables, chopped into bite-sized pieces. Each person has a small, individual bowl in which he mixes oil, salt and pepper to his own preference. He then dips his vegetables into the bowl to flavour.

Purèe: mashed and creamed vegetables, or cooked fruit.

Purslane: a small, round-leafed, herb-like plant used in salads.

Radicchio: a form of chicory or endive. It may be green or red and is eaten in salads, or grilled, baked, or used in risottos. Sharp- flavoured.

Rare: meat, grilled, fried or roast leaving the meat red and tender on the inside.

Reduce: simmer a sauce or gravy until it partially evaporates.

Ribbons: indicates the consistency of a sauce or cream when it leaves a thick, smooth trail on the surface as it falls from the spoon.

Roulade: a round 'parcel' of meat or fish, stuffed and rolled up.

Rucola: rocket. A deliciously peppery salad plant.

Schiacciata: a flat bread, marked with dimples on the surface and baked with oil and salt sprinkled on top.

Sformato: a kind of savoury pudding, not unlike the filling used in a quiche.

Skim: remove the excess fat which forms on the surface of a liquid or sauce.

Soften: fry gently until transparent and no longer crisp.

Soprassata: assorted cuts of pork, minced, chopped, dressed and flavoured in various ways, then 'pressed' into a large sausage form. Served as a cold cut meat.

Spinach, turnip greens, Swiss chard: most greengrocers sell these vegetables ready-prepared, boiled, then rolled and pressed into smallish balls.

Stew: cook slowly, simmering with liquid in a covered casserole.

Stock: liquid from stewed meats, cooked vegetables etc. used as a basis of soups, casseroles, stews.

Whisk: beat rapidly until smooth and frothy.

▼

Index

▼

▼

Contents